George Wharton James

Old missions and mission Indians of California

George Wharton James

Old missions and mission Indians of California

ISBN/EAN: 9783743496743

Manufactured in Europe, USA, Canada, Australia, Japa

Cover: Foto ©ninafisch / pixelio.de

Manufactured and distributed by brebook publishing software (www.brebook.com)

George Wharton James

Old missions and mission Indians of California

"202. San Gabriel Mission Front View. F.H.Maude photo.

B. R. Baumgardt & Co's
Old Missions
...and
Mission Indians
Of California

By

G. Wharton James, F. R. A. S.

Author of

The Lick Observatory......Tourists'
Guide Book to South California.....
From Alpine Snow to Semi=Tropic
Sea.....Nature Sermons, Etc., Etc.

Printed by B. R. Baumgardt & Co.,
Printers and Publishers, 231 West
First St., Los Angeles, California.

Beautifully Illustrated

OLD MISSIONS

AND

MISSION INDIANS

OF CALIFORNIA

FULLY ILLUSTRATED
(*Copyrighted*)

BY

G. WHARTON JAMES, F. R. A. S.

AUTHOR OF

The Lick Observatory,
Tourists' Guide Book to South California,
From Alpine Snow to Semi-Tropic Sea,
Nature Sermons, &c.

LOS ANGELES, CAL.:
B. R. BAUMGARDT & CO.
1895.

The Aged Padre at his Devotions in the Garden at Santa Barbara.

ACKNOWLEDGEMENTS.

For information on the missions I have consulted every book, magazine, or newspaper I could find, and, having drawn from such a variety of sources can do no more than make this general acknowledgement of thanks.

For the privilege of using illustrations I desire specially to thank Messrs. F. A. Pattee & Co., of the *Land of Sunshine*, B. Brooks, of the *San Luis Obispo Tribune*, C. G. Miller & Co., of the *Western Empire*, C. A. Moore, of the Los Angeles Engraving Co., Leverick A. Mesick, of *The Ojai*, T. D. Beasley, of the *Seaport News*, and C. M. Heintz, of the *Rural Californian*. To my esteemed friend, Mr. Herve Friend, I am under many obligations, both for information, photographs and engravings.

To Mr. Longley, of the Los Angeles Superior Court I am indebted for several valuable additions to my manuscript, and to my friend, Miss Nellie E. Fife, for valuable aid in preparing the index.

G. Wharton James.

Echo Mountain, Cal.
March, 1895.

NOTE.—I shall be grateful to any reader who has information not herein contained on any of the missions, if he or she will communicate it to me, and the description of any picture or relic he or she may possess or know of, in order that the second edition of this little hand book may be more accurate and complete.

THE OLD MISSIONS.

BY KIND PERMISSION.

The blue tent of the skies was spread
   Above these new-found shores,
The Future opened wide her gates,
   The old Past closed her doors;
Blossomed like stars the poppies gold,
   Which caught the sunlight sheen,
Blazing like altars on the heights,
   And sleeping vales between.

A goodly land! Her native sons
   Dreamed on the summer's breast,
Or, cradled in the sunshine, lay,
   Nursed by its warmth, at rest.
In the soft air the olive leaves,
   In silver shimmers sighed,
And the breezes blowing round them,
   In their dulcet tones replied.

Came the friars of ancient story,
   With their dusty sandals shod,
Here the holy Cross they planted,
   Longing but to worship God.
Here, beneath the oak limbs' shelter,
   First their Mission bells they swung,
And Te Deums softly chanted
   Where those sacred emblems hung.

Here the Indians gathered round them,
   Here the crucifix adored,
While the vibrant bells' sweet music
   On the sleeping air was poured,
Making echoes strange and sacred,
   Which the high stars leaned to hear,
And the rock-lipped Mounts repeated
   To the nestling canyons' ear.

One by one these hoary Missions
   With their sun-dried bricks uprose,
Holy were the hopes they signal,
   High the courage they disclose.
Hold them sacred, keep them holy,
   They are milestones on our way,
From the night of superstition
   To the broad light of Today.

                   ELIZA A. OTIS.

LIST OF ILLUSTRATIONS.

	PAGE
The Aged Padre at his Devotions in the Garden at Santa Barbara	2
The Missions of California	4
San Diego Mission with Old Palms	10
The Padre's Inspiration	11
Font at San Juan Capistrano—Bench at Los Angeles—Bells at San Juan Capistrano, San Gabriel, Pala, etc.	12
Cactus found on the way to San Diego	13
Aboriginal Woman in Ceremonial Costume	16
Aboriginal Man ready for the Chase	16
Native Indian Village	17
A Native's Winter Store of Acorns	18
An Early California Adobe	19
Tortilla Makers	20
Indian Woman Making Baskets	21
Indian Made Bench in Los Angeles Mission	22
A Mission Flock	24
Ye Men of Galilee (Music)	26
A Primitive Mission	28
Father Junipero Serra	30
Father Serra on the Shore near Monterey	34
Palms at San Diego—Steps at San Gabriel—Side Entrance and Steps at San Luis Rey	36
Sacred Lotus planted by Mission Fathers near San Diego	38
A Mission Herd in Flourishing Days	41
Palms of San Diego Mission	43
Mission of San Carlos Borromeo	46
Bells of San Carlos Borromeo	47
San Antonio de Padua	49
San Gabriel Archangel	51
"El Molino" near San Gabriel Mission	54
San Luis Obispo de Tolosa	56
The Modern City of San Luis Obispo de Tolosa	58
San Luis Obispo Entrance	60
A Primitive Indian Residence	63
Using the Metate	64
Bells and Ruined Church of San Juan Capistrano	65
In the Ruined Corridors of San Juan Capistrano	68
Triple Arch and Ruined Chapel at San Juan Capistrano	70
San Juan Capistrano Corridors	72

ILLUSTRATIONS—*Continued.*

	PAGE
San Buenaventura Mission	79
General View of San Buenaventura Mission	82
San Buenaventura Mission	83
Altar at San Buenaventura Mission	85
Santa Barbara Mission	88
Fountain and Corridors at San Fernando	100
San Fernando Rey Mission	103
San Luis Rey de Francia	105
San Luis Rey, seen through one of the Arches	106
San Luis Rey de Francia as it Originally Appeared. From an old Painting	107
San Luis Rey Mission	110
Through the Old Garden Arch at San Luis Rey	112
General View of San Luis Rey	114
Chapel and Bell Tower at San Antonio de Pala	117
Santa Ynez Mission	120
Walls of Santa Margarita Chapel	123

Errata.—By mistake the engraving on page 72 is entitled San Juan Capistrano Corridors. It should be San Luis Rey Corridors.

INDEX.

Chapter I.—Introduction—The Work of the Mission Fathers—For God and the King—Jesuits—Franciscans—Junipero Serra—Galvez—Political Results—Colonization of California—Mission Expeditions—Ship San Carlos—Padre Parron—Ship San Jose—Loss of the San Jose—The Mission Indians — Vizcaino — George Butler Griffin—Warlike Indians—Converted Indians—Work they Accomplished—Secularization—Governor Echeandia—Governor Manuel Victoria—Governor Figueroa—Condition of the Missions at Secularization—*Diezzio*—Dana's Pictures—Indian Games—Evil Results of Secularization............9 to 29

Chapter II.—Junipero Serra—His Birth—Early Educacation—Intellectual Brilliancy—His sole Ambition to Preach Christ—Work at the Apostolic College in the City of Mexico—At Sierra Gorda—Among the Apaches—In 1767 began work among the Indians of California—Results....................29 to 35

INDEX—*Continued.*

PAGE

Chapter III.—San Diego Mission.—The first of the Upper California Missions—Severe Trials on Shipboard—Zeal of Padre Serra—Portala and Father Crespi sent to find Monterey—Royal Standard Flung to the Breeze—The Country Taken for God and the King of Spain—Murder at San Diego—Death of Jose Maria—Distressing Decision of Governor Portala—Waiting for Provisions—Murder of Padre Jayme—Serra Pleads for Clemency Toward the Murderers—San Diego Mission Rebuilt—The Present Structure Erected—Prosperity of the Mission—Secularization and Its Results..35 to 45

Chapter IV.—San Carlos Borromeo.—Early Difficulties—Final Wealth and Prosperity—Recent Restoration—Serra here labored and suffered more than in any other Mission, and here he was laid to rest......................45 to 48

Chapter V.—San Antonio de Padua.—Third Mission Established—Mission founded with great enthusiasm by Serra—Rapid Growth and Prosperity—At present visited once or twice a month by a Priest from San Miguel...48 to 50

Chapter VI.—San Gabriel Archangel. — Padres Benito Cambon and Angel Somero aid Padre Serra—Mission founded on the banks of the San Gabriel River September 8, 1771—Site now marked by a few Adobe Ruins—How Reached — Present building begun 1775 — Padre Jose Maria Salvidea—Great Wealth and Prosperity of the Mission—San Gabriel the oldest Mission Building now in reasonable preservation — Cactus Hedges—Old Mill Buildings—Still a fairly large population of Mexicans—Regular services kept up...............................50 to 55

Chapter VII.—San Luis Obispo De Tolosa.—Established 1772—Padre Cavaller in charge—Friendly feeling of the natives—A year of struggle followed by prosperity—Buildings burned three times—Tile roofs—Padre Luis Martinez—Story of " H. H." illustrating the character of Martinez—Buildings injured by the earthquake of 1812—How reached..55 to 61

Chapter VIII.—San Francisco De Assis.—Founded October 9, 1776—"Mission Dolores"—Padre Serra's visit and confirmation of first converts, 1781—General Vallejo's statements regarding the work of the Padres—In 1826 the Mission still in splendor—Changes wrought in a hundred years—Industrial work—Government of the Indians...61 to 64

Chapter IX.—San Juan Capistrano.—Founded November 1, 1776, by President Serra—Work begun the previous year—Delay on account of murder at San Diego—

INDEX—*Continued.*

PAGE

Earnestness of the San Juan Indians—Rapid growth—Destruction by the earthquake of 1812—Beauty of the ruins — Patriotic recollections—Architecture—Traditions—Secularization of 1833 — Micheltorena— Mission purchased by James McKinley and John Foster—Naming of the Mission by Portala—Accommodations for tourists—Hot Springs—How reached...64 to 74

Chapter X.—Santa Clara.—Founded by Padre Tomas de la Pena, 1777—Pena and Murguia in charge—Floods—Removal to higher ground—Beauty of the buildings—Death of Murguia—Present structure built in 1825-6—Exciting and interesting events—Yoscolo—Revolt and escape—Stanislaus' revolt—Vallejo in pursuit—Battle and final capture of Yoscolo—In 1839 Estrada gives away or sells the Mission lands—Ruin and decay...................74 to 78

Chapter XI.—San Buenaventura.—Serra's determination to found a chain of Missions between San Diego and Santa Barbara —Political changes and complications—Three Missions to be founded near the Santa Barbara Channel—Portala visits the coast—Indians more industrious than elsewhere—Builders, fishermen, workers in wood, stone, etc.—Permission of Governor Neve to found the Missions at Santa Barbara and San Buenaventura—Serra's visit to the Channel Indians—Expedition to and founding of San Buenaventura—Rapid growth in the early part of this century—Padres Dumetz and Maria gladdened by many accessions—Finer flocks and herds, fields, gardens and orchards than in any of the Missions—Battle between Carrillo and Alvarado in 1838—Father Rubio now in charge—Renovation in 1893—The present building—Impressive rededication in 1894...78 to 87

Chapter XII—Santa Barbara.—Presidio and Mission, Founded 1782—Governor Neve and the Soldiers Assist Serra at the Dedication—Delay in Erecting the Buildings—Death of Padre Serra—Father Palou made President of the Missions—Padre Lasuen Succeeds Him in 1786—Mission Established—Padres Paterna and Oramas in Charge—The Buildings—Plundering of the Missions—Secularization did Less Damage than in Other Missions—In Possession of the Franciscans—In 1853 it became a Hospice—In 1885 it Became a Part of the "Province of the Sacred Heart of Jesus"—Interest Attaching to the Mission—Visits of Princess Louise and Mrs. President Harrison—Kindness of Res dent Padres....................87 to 92

Chapter XIII—La Purisima Conception.—Third of the Channel Missions—Early Buildings—Earthquake and

INDEX—*Continued.*

PAGE

Flood—Padre Payeras—His Buildings, Zeal, Converts, etc.—Secularization in 1835—Governor Pico's Proclamation in 1844—Buildings Restored to the Catholic Church...92 to 93

Chapter XIV—Santa Cruz.—Founded by Padre Lasuen 1791—Second Child of the San Francisco Mission—Sugert, the Indian Chief—1834-5, Del Valle Appointed Comisionado—Robbing of the Indians—In 1856 the Ruins Desecrated by Treasure Seekers.....................94 to 95

Chapter XV—La Soledad.—Its History Little Known — Its Indian Name "Chattusgelis"—Named by Portala "Soledad"..95 to 96

Chapter XVI—San Jose.—Founded by Padre Lasuen 1796 or 1797—Padre Borcenilla and Merino in Charge—Romantic Side—Rich Lands—Trapping Done by the Indians —Stanislaus Educated Here—His Raid—Vallejo's Discipline—Wealth of the Mission When he Took Possession—Ruins Much Visited and Painted.............................96 to 97

Chapter XVII—San Juan Bautista.—Founded 1797— Present Buildings Erected 1800—Spanish Name "Benito" Indians Called it "Popeloutchom"—In a Wide and Beautiful Valley—Buildings—Bells......................97 to 98

Chapter XVIII - San Miguel.—"Sagshpilesl"—Founded in 1797—Padre Sitjar Presents Fifteen Children for Baptism—Rapid Growth—Conversion of Guchapa—Force Used to Gain Converts—San Miguel Never as Prosperous as Some of the Other Missions—Small Crops—Required to Send Supplies to Mexican Troops—San Miguel Celebrated by Ross Browne in "Dangerous Journey"— Only One of Its Three Bells remains......................98 to 101

Chapter XIX—San Fernando.—Chain of Missions from San Diego to Monterey—San Fernando Founded September 8th, 1797—Present Building Dedicated 1806—Located in a Most Fertile Valley—The Granary of Los Angeles County—Buildings and Scenery—Flourishing Condition in 1820—Mission Sold in 1846 to Help Toward War Expenses—Gold First Discovered at San Fernando in 1846—Richness of the Mines—The Misson Now in an Utterly Ruined Condition...................................101 to 104

Chapter XX—San Luis Rey de Francia.—Founded June 13th, 1798—Regarded as "King of the Missions"— Five Padres, Serra, Palou, Crespi, Salvidea and Peyri— The Present Structure Built in 1802—Beauty and Fertility of the Location—Great Wealth and Prosperity—Ruins Majestic and Imposing—Secularization and Departure of Father Peyri—Memory of Padre Salvidea—His Devotions

INDEX—*Continued.*

PAGE

and Eccentricities—The Love of the People for Him—In 1892 the Work of Repairing the Mission Begun Under Father O'Keefe—May 12th, 1893, the Re-dedication Occurred—Impressive Ceremonies—The Renovated Buildings—Visit to the Mission........................104 to 115

Chapter XXI.—San Antonio de Pala.—Not Properly a Mission, only a Chapel—Picturesque Belfry—Its two Bells still call the Indians to Worship——The Building—Indian Settlement near Pala—The Building Guarded by two old Indians—Statues—Accommodations for Tourists....115 to 118

Chapter XXII.—Santa Ynez—Founded for the Convenience of the Rancheros in 1804—First Church shattered by the Earthquake of 1812—New Building dedicated July 4, 1819—Decline—Rebellion and Murder................118 to 119

Chapter XXIII.—San Rafael.—Lieutenant Sola's Suggestion—Founded in 1817... 119

Chapter XXIV.—San Francisco Solano—Founded April 4, 1824—Now Disappeared... 121

Chapter XXV.—Los Angeles Chapel – Authority gained for its Erection in 1811—August 1814 Foundation Stone laid—Site changed in 1818—1822 formerly Dedicated...... 121

Chapter XXVI.—Santa Margarita Chapel—Why Built—Now in Ruins—J. Ross Browne ....122 to 124

Chapter XXVII.—"Cui Bono?"—What is the good of it all?—Dwinelle's words—Society for the Preservation of the Missions 124

The Padre's Inspiration.

OLD MISSIONS AND MISSION INDIANS OF CALIFORNIA.

CHAPTER I.

INTRODUCTION.

Pathos, tragedy, comedy, courage, heroism, aspirations, conflict, triumph, defeat, despair, loss, are all written in unfading letters across the horizon of the Spanish missionary enterprises of California. Ignatius Loyola was not more devoted to his order and the Jesus he believed in, than Junipero Serra and his coadjutors were in their mission work and the Jesus they sought to present to the aborigines of this sun-lit but ignorance-cursed region. Elsewhere I have spoken of the emotions the sight of the ruined adobe structures the mission fathers left should awaken in the hearts of the thoughtful and earnest. The picture of Junipero Serra led Helen Hunt Jackson to exclaim: "Ah! faithful, noble, dear old face; what an unselfish, devoted life you led! All I ask is to be permitted to meet you in the other world."

These ruined churches, then, are beautiful and worthy reminders of beautiful and worthy lives,— lives consecrated for the uplifting of those who knew not the joys of the true Christian believer.

San Diego Mission with Old Palms

It will be impossible of course, in the brief space of a few pages, to give such full and complete accounts ot the founding and history of the missions as both author and reader would like. To the interested reader the author must refer him to his large and beautifully illustrated work on the missions now in course of preparation, and which he hopes very shortly to publish.

FOR GOD AND THE KING.

In 1767, King Charles III. of Spain ordered an expedition to sail, to take possession of the Californias, convert the Indians found there, and protect the country from the encroachments of Russians from the north, which the latter then owned. Jose de Galvez, the visitador general of New Spain,—a man of great foresight and ability,—to whom the Americans of the South California of to-day owe much,—was the man to whom this important undertaking was intrusted. The only knowledge of where he was to go was obtained from the very indefinite "survey" of Vizcaino, "yet so closely was this first definite scheme of colonization and conversion planned that there were orders to plant a mission and garrison first at San Diego, then at Monterey, and then one, half way between, to be called Buena Ventura."

Shortly before this expedition was organized the Jesuits, who had founded a number of missions in Baja California, were expelled from Mexico, and their work was placed under the control of the Franciscans, with headquarters at the College of San Fernando, in the City of Mexico. The College, with a perspicacity highly commendable, chose Padre Junipero Serra as the President of these missions, and when Galvez required of them missionaries to accompany him on his expedition north, Serra's jurisdiction was extended, and he was appointed president of all the California missions, those already in existence in Lower Cali-

Font at San Juan Capistrano—Bench at Los Angeles—Bells at San Juan Capistran San Gabriel, Pala, &c.

Cactus found on the way to San Diego

fornia and those to be founded in Upper California. The following pages deal entirely with the work of Serra and his religious coadjutors. But the work of Galvez was so important and far-reaching in its results as to demand a little enlarging upon. He was the practical head of the expedition, ordering the taking with it of 200 head of cattle from the northernmost mission of Lower California, and also of a full supply of all kinds of seeds of vegetables, grains and flowers; everything, in fact, that grew in Old Spain he wished transplanted to New Spain. "It was he, also, as full of interest for chapel as for farm, who selected and packed with his own hands sacred ornaments and vessels for church ceremonies. A curious letter of his to Father Palou is extant in which he says, laughingly, that he is a better sacristan than Father Junipero, having packed the holy vessels and ornaments quicker and better than he."

This expedition, from a political standpoint, definitely placed California under the rule of Spain, under which it remained until Mexico declared her independence, in 1822, and made California a portion of her territory. During this period of the Franciscans, San Diego: Los Angeles, San Juan Capistrano, San Luis Rey, San Gabriel, San Buenaventura, San Luis Obispo, San Fernando, San Pedro and Santa Barbara pueblos or towns, were all founded.

To the practical mind the chief significance, possibly, of the founding of the missions is that the padres first began the colonization of California.

THE MISSION EXPEDITIONS.

On the 9th of January, 1769, the ship San Carlos set sail, Padre Parron, one of Serra's missionaries being of the party.

On the 15th of February the San Antonio sailed from Cape San Lucas, and on the 16th of June still another boat, the San Jose, sailed.

The land division of the expedition was also divided into two parts. One section, commanded by Rivera, a captain of the Company of Cuera (or leather jacket) left Santa Ana in Lower California in September, 1768. After a long delay at Vellicata in Lower California, fifty days journeying brought them to San Diego, and there they found the San Carlos and the San Antonio at anchor. The San Jose never did appear and was undoubtedly lost at sea with all hands.

Before starting himself in the second section of the land expedition Serra founded the Mission of San Fernando at Vellicata and then, accompanied by Portala, the royally appointed Governor of California, the expedition started. After forty-six days' journey from the newly founded San Fernando chapel, on July 1, 1769, Serra reached San Diego.

THE MISSION INDIANS.

Who the Indians were, that afterward became known only as the "Mission Indians," is not an easy question to determine. There have been many attempts at a solution of the problem, and antiquarians are still vexing themselves and each other by their sage conjectures and wild guesses.

Of their Aboriginal history but little is known. There are many conflicting reports about the primitive people. The subject is exhaustively discussed by Hubert Howe Bancroft in his "Native Races of the Pacific Coast."

Vizcaino says he found the land "thickly settled with people who were of gentle disposition, peaceable and docile, and who can be brought readily within the fold of the holy gospel and into subjection to the Crown of Your Majesty. Their food consists of seeds which they have in abundance and variety, and of the flesh of game, such as deer which are larger than cows, and bear, and of neat cattle and bisons and many other animals. The Indians are of good stature and fair complexion, the women being somewhat less in size than the men and of pleasing countenance. The clothing of the people of the coast-lands consists of the skins of the sea-wolves abounding there, which they tan and dress better than is done in Castile. * * * * * They have vessels of pine-wood very well

The Aboriginal Woman in Ceremonial Costume

The Aboriginal Man Ready for the Chase

made, in which they go to sea with fourteen paddle-men on a side, with great dexterity—even in very stormy weather. I was informed by them, and by many others I met with in great numbers along more than eight hundred leagues of a thickly settled coast, that inland there are great communities, which they invited me to visit with them. They manifested great friendship for us and a desire for intercourse; were well affected toward the image of Our Lady which I showed to them, and very attentive to the sacrifice of the mass. They worship different idols, and they are well acquainted with silver and gold, and said that these were found in the interior.''

But George Butler Griffin, the translator of this and other letters of Vizcaino, says in a foot-note that "Vizcaino's letters, generally, are full of exaggerated statements and falsehoods, and in this letter he gives his fancy a slack rein. * * * * At the time of his visit many of the beasts and plants he mentions did not exist, nor had they ever existed, in California; nor did he meet with any natives such as he describes.''

Native Indian Village

I think it may be relied upon that the native Indians of California varied in habits, character and war-likeness, as the Indians of Arizona vary to-day. There are the Pueblo Indians—a commercial, home-loving, industrious, peaceable race; the Hualpais, a degraded and sensual people; the warlike, bloodthirsty and cruel Apaches, who have been the terror of settlers for many years, until the final capture and deportation of the leaders; the silver working Navajoes, and several others.

The Indians who roamed in the mountains to the East of San Diego were a more adventurous, daring and warlike people than the pastoral Indians found in the valleys and pasture lands nearer Los Angeles. There were the degraded "Diggers" and the intelligent Temecula tribes. A mixed lot, some good, some fair, and some, as the good Indians themselves would designate them, "no good."

"The natives were timid in their intercourse with the strangers whom they called Guaccunal, but they wounded with their arrows those of a party that landed at night to fish. Interviews, voluntary and enforced, were held with a few individuals both on shore and on

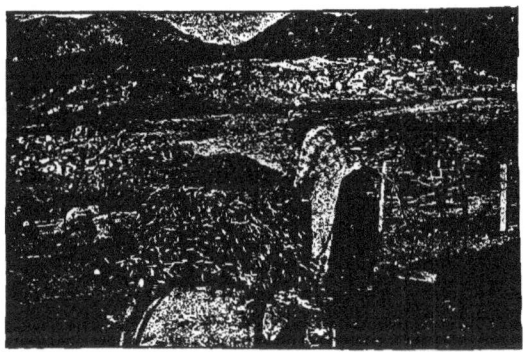

A Native's Winter Store of Acorns

the ships; and the Spaniards understood by their signs that the natives had seen or heard of men like themselves, bearded, mounted and armed, somewhere in the interior. It is neither impossible, nor improbable, that the natives had heard of Diaz, Alarcon, and Ulloa at the head of the gulf. The Indians of San Diego are described 'as well formed, of large size and clothed in skins.'"

THE CONVERTED INDIANS.

In 1780, the sixteen padres of California had 3,000 converts under their control. In 1800, this number had increased to 13,500, with eighteen missions and forty padres. And when it is remembered that of this rude, ignorant, useless, savage population the padres made "silleros (saddlers), herreros (blacksmiths), sastres (tailors), molineros (millers), panaderos (bakers), plateros (silversmiths), toneleros (coopers), cargadores (freighters), valeros (candle makers), vendemiadores (vintagers), caldereros (coppersmiths), zapateros (shoemakers), sombrereros (hatters), comfeleros de panocha (makers of panocha), guitarreros (guitarmakers), arrieros (muleteers), alcaldes, mayordomos,

An Early California Adobe.

rancheros (ranchmen), medicos (doctors), pastores (shepherds), cordileros (ropemakers), leñadores (woodcutters), pentores (painters), esculores (sculptors), albaniles (masons), toreadores (toreadors), acolitos (acolytes), canteros (stonecutters), sacristanes (sacristans), campaneros (bellringers), cocineros (cooks), cantores (singers), musicos (musicians), cazadores (hunters), jaboneros (soapmakers), curtidores (tanners), tegidores (weavers), tigeros (tilemakers), bordodores (embroiderers), pescatores (fishermen), marineros (sailors), vineteros (winemakers), caporales (corporals), habradores (farmers), vaqueros (herders), llaveros

The Tortilla Makers

(turnkeys), domadores (horse-tamers), barberos (barbers), cesteros (basket-makers), and carpenteros (carpenters), with European models, standards and methods, the wonder at the marvellous power of the the padres grows into a reverence.

Wood and stone carving, engraving of horn, inlaying of wood and of iron with silver, leather work, the embossing of shields and saddles, silver work, basket making, lace and drawn work, hair work, frescoing, rude painting, embroidering in gold and

Indian Made Bench, in Los Angeles Mission

silver thread, and the making of musical instruments —all these arts were gradually practiced under favorable conditions for developing individual capacity. Indians made, in mortar, vats for the wine, fountains for the water, zanjas for irrigation, the covering of walls for defence. In wood, they carved statues, stirrups, fonts, pulpits, chairs, benches, doorways and altar-rails. They made sun-dials and the stocks ; the varas de justica, or sticks of justice, carried by the mayordomos; the esposas or manacles for refractory neophytes; brands for the tithed mission herds; book-covers and sandals for the padres; tuna and pomegranate wine; panocha for the children; mail for the soldiers; biers for the dead."

I say, when it is remembered that such a host of skilled workers and producers were developed by the sagacious training of the savages by the padres, California owes much, in the way of its advancement, to these missionary laborers. Spread the glory of these achievements! Never was there in any land such a record of accomplishment in so brief a period.

SECULARIZATION.

In 1830, Governor Echeandia, who was opposed to the missions, succeeded in getting the California legislature to pass an act, providing for their gradual transformation into pueblos, and for making each Indian a shareholder in the lands and cattle. But before this plan could be put in operation it was necessary that it be confirmed by the home government in Mexico, and before this could be done Echeandia was succeeded in the Gubernatorial office by Manuel Victoria, who had for some time been governor of Lower California.

The rule of Victoria was unproductive of any good results, as far as the missions were concerned, except for a short time to arrest the coming of the secularization tornado.

In 1833, General Jose Figueroa, was appointed Governor, and under his rule the unexpected blow was struck.

Though himself a conservative man, and opposed to anything more than the gradual emancipation of the neophytes of the missions, the dread order of secularization, so long feared by the padres, was passed by the Mexican Congress August 17, 1833.

A brief statement here of the material condition of the missions will not be out of place, together with vivid pictures by eye witnessess of methods of conducting business at the missions, both before and after the secularization. I quote now from James Steele's "Old California Days." "Seven hundred thousand cattle grazed on the mission pastures, with sixty thousand horses and an immense number of other domestic animals.

"A hundred and twenty thousand bushels of wheat were raised annually, besides other crops.

A Mission Flock

"The usual products came under the following heads: wheat, wine, brandy, soap, leather, hides, wool, oil, cotton, hemp, linen, tobacco, salt, soda.

"Two hundred thousand head of cattle were slaughtered annually, at a net profit of ten dollars each.

"Gardens, vineyards and orchards surrounded or were contiguous to all the missions except the two most northern ones.   *   *   *   *   *

"The total average annual gains of the missions from sales and trade generally were more than two million dollars. This, on an uninhabited and distant coast where commerce, in our sense, was unknown. "The value of the live stock alone, was, in 1834, two millions of dollars."

William Heath Davis says: "The missions exacted from the cattle owners as contribution, known as *dieznio*, for the support and benefit of the clergy, and for the expense of the missions, one-tenth of the increase of the cattle. The tax was not imposed by the general government, but was solely an ecclesiastical matter, diligently collected by the clergy of the different missions, and religiously contributed by the rancheros."

DANA'S PICTURE OF THE LAND.

Dana, in his "Two Years Before the Mast," draws a number of fascinating pictures of the state of the country in the years 1835-6. Of Santa Barbara he says:

"The town lies a little nearer to the beach, about half a mile from it, and is composed of one-story houses, built of sun-dried clay, or *adobe*, some of them whitewashed, with red tiles on the roofs. I should judge that there were about a hundred of them; and in the midst of them stands the Presidio, or fort, built of the same materials, and apparently but little stronger. The town is finely situated, with a bay in front and an amphitheater of hills behind. The only thing which diminishes its beauty is that the hills have no large trees upon them, they having been all burnt by a great fire which swept them off about a dozen years ago, and they had not yet grown again. The fire was described to me by an inhabitant, as having been a very terrible and magnificent sight. The air of the whole valley was so heated that the

people were obliged to leave the town and take up their quarters for several days upon the beach."

In his chapter on San Diego he thus describes a portion of one of his Sundays:

INDIAN GAMES.

"The Indians, who always have a holiday on Sunday, were engaged at playing a kind of running game of ball, on a level piece of ground, near the houses. The old ones sat down in a ring, looking on, while the young ones—men, boys and girls—were chasing the ball, and throwing it with all their might. Some of the girls ran like greyhounds. At every accident, or remarkable feat, the old people set up a deafening screaming and clapping of hands. Several bluejackets were reeling about among the houses, which showed that the pulperias had been well patronized. One or two of the sailors had got on horseback, but being rather indifferent horsemen, and the Mexicans having given them vicious beasts, they were soon thrown, much to the amusement of the people. A half-dozen Sandwich Islanders, from the hide-houses and the two brigs, bold riders, were dashing about on a full gallop, hallooing and laughing like so many wild men."

SECULARIZATION.

When the padres saw that the political tornado of spoilation was coming upon the missions, they began, at once, to convert all their cattle and stock, as far as possible, into money. General M. G. Vallejo is authority for the statement that "in the missions of San Gabriel, San Fernando, San Juan Capistrano and San Luis Rey, they killed by contract with private individuals, during the years 1830, 1831 and 1832, more than sixty thousand head of cattle, from which they only saved the hides. The pecuniary wealth of the missions in their primitive days, which were more productive, was sent out of the country to Spain,

Mexico or Italy. This I know; and presume, and even believe, that all of it arrived safely at its place of destination.''

Thus the mission property wasted away. Many of the padres returned to Mexico, and the neophytes, for whose good they had labored with so much care, were scattered in the towns and villages of the gentiles, to whom the mission lands were granted by the authorities.

For a long time the country suffered by the absence of the guiding hands of the padres, but by and bye, the recuperative energy of the region manifested itself. The new comers were incited to labor intelligently by the stories of the successes of the priests, and it is asserted, upon good authority, that even after the secularization of the missions and consequent dispersion of their property, that California "in proportion to the population, was the richest of any country under Spanish dominion and inhabited by citizens of Castilian extraction.''

From this period dates the want of care of the mission buildings. They were unsalable, the padres had no one to care for them; some of them were deserted, and so they began to crumble, until to-day so many of them are found in a state of utter dilapidation and ruin.

CHAPTER II.

JUNIPERO SERRA.

It is appropriate in considering these Missions and their work that we endeavor to gain some conception of the personality of Junipero Serra, the brave Franciscan missionary, who was the chief spiritual director of the whole undertaking.

He was born at Petra, in the Isle of Majorca, Nov. 24, 1713, became a novice on the 14th of Sept., 1730, and entered a convent at Palma, the capital of Majorca.

At this time he became fired with earnest zeal for the cause of missions. He wrote, "During my

Father Junipero Serra

studies I had a most ardent desire to leave my country and go among the Indians; I took a resolution to that effect."

On the 15th of September, 1731, he professed, and was soon afterwards transferred to another convent, where he studied philosophy and theology. Such was his scholarship and ardor, that, even before he was ordained, he was made Professor of Philosophy, and before the end of his studies of the philosophical curriculum, received the title of D. D.

He excelled as an orator, and literary men listened to him, fascinated by the clear brilliancy of his style, and the forcefulness of his utterance. One of his enemies once said, himself a famous orator: "This sermon is worth being printed in letters of gold."

And yet he had no other ambition than to preach Christ to the rude peasants, or to go and bury himself among the uncivilized children of the forest.

His wish was to be fulfilled. In 1749, August 28th, he set sail, with others, from his convent of Palma, and on the 7th of December reached Vera Cruz, and, on New Year's Day, 1750, he entered the Apostolic College of San Fernando, in the City of Mexico.

It was not long before his restless spirit asserted itself, and the Guardian of the College sent him and Father Palou to work among the aborigines of Sierra Gorda. "This rugged place is situated at the distance of thirty leagues from Inerataro, but is over one hundred leagues in extent."

Just as he was beginning to enjoy the fruit of hard labor among these people, he was called to engage in the conquest of souls among the treacherous and warlike Apaches. His predecessors had been ill treated and finally murdered, but, without a murmur, he prepared for his journey, when news arrived that plans were altered, so, obeying the voice of his superiors, he retired to his convent. From this place he occupied himself constantly in Missions here, there and everywhere, astonishing all by his tireless energy, and never-ceasing labors for the good of others.

Then, in 1767, came the order for him to take command of the spiritual work among the Indians of California.

The result of these labors is well known. Loving, zealous, indefatigable, he labored and toiled, until God called him to a well-earned reward. He died at the Mission of San Carlos, August 28, 1784, at the age of 70 years, 9 months and four days.

Of his work, these pages are a brief and inadequate record.

At his death his life-long friend, Father Palou, said of him:

> "Here 's one of whom posterity will say,
> ' He was the greatest man that ever trod
> The sands of Alta California.' "
>
> "*Father Junipero Serra*," *Act IV, Scene II.*

and I believe in the truth of what his fellowmen said of him:

> "To pass him in his loftiness of thought,
> Excel him in the greatness of his works,
> Exceed him in his pious kindness,
> Transcend his deep devotion to our God,
> Or still display more energy than he;
> One could not do."
>
> "*Father Junipero Serra*," *Act II, Scene II.*

The best that any man can do is to spell out, live out as best he may the ideas that impel him from within. Some do this well, some do it ill, *but that they do it* is the matter of greatest importance. Padre Serra was impelled, taken possession of, by the idea that these California savages were lost, irretrievably and forever damned unless some one preached Christ to them.

The theology of Dante was a real, terrible, absorbing truth to him. Only to such a belief was such work as his possible. Hell, with its dire circles of horror and terror for those who were unbelievers in the Christ he worshipped, yawned before the feet of these untamed and rude California savages. Properly trained into a knowledge of the church and its saving ordinances by an apostolic guide, there was a new hereafter presented to them. Purgatory was open, and from thence, duly purged from their sin and ignorance, they might climb into the blessed regions of Paradise. Felicity untold, then, to that man who would brave their savagery, dare their treachery, love them even in their unloveableness, and thus lead them into the fold of the church.

Who should do it? Should he, with his soul athirst for great deeds, full of bravery and heroism, stand by, in order to listen to the applause of his civilized world as his words of burning eloquence pleased his ears, and let some half-hearted, half-in-earnest priest go out to these degraded savages? No! The greater their need and danger the greater the necessity for speed, power and earnestness in the one who should go to them. So, leaving the world and its vain applause, society and its pettings, civilization and its luxurious comforts, casting all these things behind him, he gladly, joyfully and yet seriously, started out to do the bidding of his superiors.

"Narrow," some of my readers may say he was! His theological conceptions crude and bigoted! So were Dante's, but that did not prevent him from giving the Divine Commedia to the world. And Milton, too, could not be truthfully designated broad, in the modern theological sense, yet Paradise Lost will live when much of the "broad" trash of these days has sunk into the "backward of time" and been forgotten.

No more humble man was it possible to find. Even a shell in his eyes was a marvelous work, and the theme of a sermon. In his Historical Drama, Mr. C. G. Miller makes him say:

"Last night I found upon the sandy beach
    An abalone shell, the sea had thrown
    From off the rocks, the place where it had grown.
That lustrous nacre as it lay to bleach,
Gave me a theme that I to all could preach;
    It was, ' How little are God's wonders known,'
    On every side so lavish has He sown,
Yet on we pass, quite heedless what's in reach.

Then sad became my thoughts there on the sand,
  While restless waves their nocturnes moaned to me;
For that bright pearl made by our Father's hand,
  Disclosed that I, of intellect so free,
Could at my death leave not one work so grand,
  As was that shell left strandeded by the sea."

Father Serra on the shore near Monterey.

There was something about the man Serra that demanded and gained the sincere homage of these savages. A senseless theory it would be to make it out that he merely conquered them by force of arms and then by intimidation kept them in a state of subjection. Such an explanation were unworthy one who knows anything of the Indian character,—his natural repugnance to anything that savors of physical domination.

Is Serra lost, dead? Can such a man ever be lost, ever be dead? Serra had too great an influence, transient through to us it now seems, ever to be lost.

He is found in us, lives yet in the impulse he gives us to nobleness of life, unselfishness, devotion to the lowest and the most degraded—a teacher to us of the grandeur of service, of the majesty of human character when guided, controlled, dominated by wise and purposeful love for his needy fellows. I say wise and purposeful love! There is much that calls itself love that is neither wise nor purposeful. If you would help the poor and needy, help them by a love that is wise for them and for you, and is full of purpose,— purpose that can never be swerved from its attainment—a purpose kept faithful unto death.

CHAPTER III.

SAN DIEGO MISSION.

This was the first of the Upper California missions. It was founded July 16, 1769, by Padre Junipero Serra. The circumstances surrounding the foundation were of an especially affecting and interesting character. It was the beginning of the realization of Padre Serra's fondest hopes. His zealous heart was full of enthusiasm when he started, but on his arrival at San Diego the horrible condition of the crews of the two vessels that awaited his arrival was such as to dampen the most fiery ardor and quell the enthusiasm of the most dauntless. Insufficient and unwholesome food, bad water, poor sanitary conditions, a four months' journey had produced scurvy on board both ships, and fifteen days after Junipero Serra's arrival twenty-nine sailors and soldiers were dead. "The Indians, who at first had been gentle and friendly,

grew each day more insolent and thievish, even tearing off the clothes of the sick lying helpless in the tents or tule huts on the beach."

Yet with zeal kept ablaze by faith and trust in God, Serra sent off, on the 14th of July, Portala the Governor and Father Crespi, to find Monterey, and two days later, with a cross erected, facing the port, and in a rude booth of branches and reeds, in the presence of sailors and soldiers, Serra said mass. The bell was rung hanging suspended from the boughs of a tree; the whole congregation sang the "Veni Creator;" the royal standard was flung to the breeze; the water was blessed; the awe-stricken Indians watching the mysterious proceedings with profound attention and astonished curiosity; firearms were discharged to supply the want of an organ, and "the smoke of muskets ascended for incense;" and thus the ceremony was performed and the country taken "for God and the King of Spain."

MURDER AT SAN DIEGO.

On the 15th of August, Padre Junipero had just finished the celebration of the mass, when some Indians, armed with arrows, wooden sabres and clubs, fell upon the missionaries. The corporal, with the four soldiers who had been left as a guard, at once gave the alarm and began to fire on their attackers, when Father Vizcaino, raising the mat of his hut to see if anyone was killed, received an arrow wound in the hand. At the same moment his servant, named Jose Maria, rushed in, and, falling at his feet cried: "Father, absolve me; I have been mortally wounded." The father did so, and in a few moments the soul of the first South California martyr had winged its flight to heaven. How many of the Indians were killed is not known, but in a few days they brought their wounded to be cared for at the mission. Fortunately Padre Serra was unhurt, and by the exercise of that loving

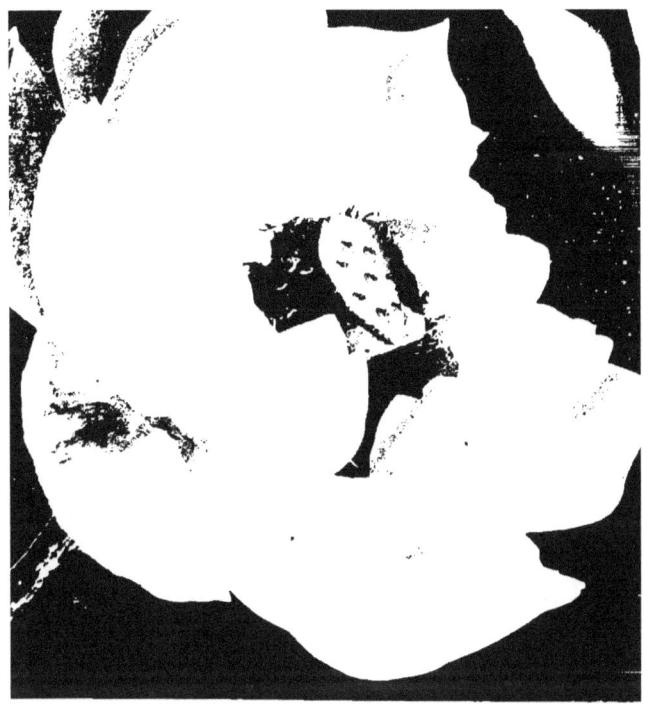

The Sacred Lotus. Planted by the Mission Fathers near San Diego

patience and forbearance which characterized his life he soon won the regard of the Indians.

On January 24, 1770, the expedition which had gone north to found other missions, returned. Governor Portala, seeing the supply of provisions rapidly diminishing, saddened the heart of Serra by informing him that if he did not receive fresh supplies from San Blas before the 19th of March he would be compelled to abandon the San Diego mission and return. As the fateful day approached, and no vessel came, despondency fell upon the priests, but Serra continued to pray, and we are told that "towards evening the fog, which had enshrouded the bay all day, vanished, and, lo! far away, a ship was descried approaching the harbor, but was soon again lost to view." This apparition, or whatever it was, induced Portala to hold out a little longer, and four days later the "San Antonio" entered the bay amid rejoicings and pious acclaim. These events transpired at the spot where the ruins of the old presidio are now found, near the "Old Town" of San Diego. When the presidio and other military buildings were completed Padre Serra moved, in 1774, the mission two leagues away, to a place called "Nipaguay."

MURDER OF PADRE JAYME AT SAN DIEGO.

Five years later, the new site was watered with the blood of a murdered missionary. On the 3rd of October, 1775, Fathers Luis Jayme and Vincent Fuster baptized sixty Indians. This so aroused the enmity of some of the Indian leaders that, emboldened by the six miles distance of the presidio, there assembled a large number, over 1,000, Indians of different tribes, and, on the night of the 4th of November, marched to the attack. One party was to destroy the mission, and the other the presidio. Their plans were well laid. The mission building was fired, the church pillaged, and, armed with arrows and *macanas*, a kind of wooden sword shaped like a cimitar, they proceeded to hunt for the missionaries. Father Vincent Fuster escaped, but Father Jayme who slept in another building, seeing the conflagration, rushed out, and meeting a large group of Indians greeted them with the usual salutation: "Let us love God, my children." Immediately they rushed upon him with wolflike ferocity, dragged him to the creek, and, after stripping him of his gown, they beat him, shot him with many arrows, and, after he was dead, bruised and mutilated him until nothing but his hands were recognizable.

Until daybreak these howling and ferocious devils surrounded the remaining priest, soldiers and laborers, every now and again, the corporal, who was a sharpshooter, killing or wounding one of them.

In the morning they fled, when the Christian Indians, who had been confined during the attack, came out and with tears and lamentations discovered their dead priest. The blacksmith also was killed, and five days later the carpenter, Ursulino, died.

Instead of seeking vengence upon the bloody murderers of his co-worker, Padre Serra pleaded with the military governor, while strengthening their force at San Diego, to show clemency to the misguided Indians. The Viceroy gave instructions to that effect, so, instead of provoking these ignorant savages to greater cruelties and outbreaks, Padre Serra was left to win them, in his own way, by tenderness and love. Orders were also given to rebuild the Mission of San Diego, which was accordingly accomplished in 1776-7, twelve soldiers being detailed by Captain Rivera as a guard to protect the workmen engaged upon it. The building was dedicated November 12, 1777, but was not entirely completed until the year 1784.

In 1804 a new church was built, and in 1813 the structure was erected, the ruins of which arrest the attention of the traveler to-day. This building was

dedicated November 12, 1813, with great solemnity. It stands on an eminence, at a point in the valley of the San Diego River which commands a fine view of the entire valley to the sea on the one side, and of the mountains on the other. The main building is about ninety feet long, and extends from north to south, the main entrance being at the south end. The massive walls, about four feet in thickness, are built of adobe, the doorways and windows being made of burnt tiles.

"According to the census reported to the Viceroy in the year 1800, the Presidio of San Diego had a population of 167, consisting of officers and soldiers, and their families. They possessed 820 head of cattle and 403 head of horses. The mission then had within its premises an Indian population of 1501, and the Fathers owned 6,000 head of cattle and about the same number of sheep, and 877 head of horses. In that year (1800) the Mission raised 3,000 bushels of wheat and 2,000 bushels of barley. In 1827 the Mission possessed 17,284 head of sheep, 9,120 head of cattle and 1,123 head of horses."

By the decree of Secularization all this was scattered and now nothing but the dilapidated ruins remain of the once proud and flourishing mission of San Diego.

The visitor to San Diego Mission will immediately notice the large palms, just a little distance below the ruins. These proud and ancient trees, though not so weighed down with antiquity as the pyramids, have yet seen many and wonderful changes in the more-than-a-hundred years since they were planted. They saw the early days of the mission; often listened to Padre Serra's voice, as he pleaded with the Indians to be won to Christ and Holy Church; witnessed the sad murder of Padre Jayme, and the fearful uprising of the infuriated savages; were silent listeners to the hopes and fears of Serra after Portala had informed him that the mission must be abandoned; saw the welcome growth of interest in the hearts of the aborigines; the

Palms of San Diego Mission

earliest baptisms; the enlarged services; the busy throngs of converts; heard the glad songs of praise of priests and neophytes; and finally saw the effect of the sad decree of secularization.

A great and eventful history all to transpire under the notice of these trees.

Whether the palm is indigenous to the soil of California, or is an importation brought hither by the same forethought that "brought sheep, cattle and all kinds of seeds," is a disputed question. The existence of the groves of palms, in Palm Valley, under the giant shoulder of Mount San Jacinto, is offered in evidence that the palm is indigenous. But it is easily possibly that these palms are the result of the planting of one or two of the species near the Hot Springs, which were assuredly visited early in Mission history by the enterprising and indefatigable padres.

However this may be, the palm is a prominent and important feature of almost every mission ruin, and one cannot fail to observe them with enlarged interest after remembering their connection with the historical works of the padres.

Alongside the ruins of San Diego Mission is a modern building, recently erected, for the education of the Indian girls of the neighborhood. With a devotion, equalled only by that of the earlier missionaries, Father Ubach has given his life to the work of caring for and training these girls into the ways of helpful civilization and Christianity, and with uniformly good results.

This is another instance of what I shall elsewhere call attention to, viz., the fact that these old missions, or their sites, are now being utilized for the education of either the neighboring people or of those who will aid in propagating the Catholic faith.

To reach this mission the visitor can proceed direct to San Diego, on the Surf Line of the Santa Fe System, and there engage a carriage to drive him out.

The distance is some five or six miles from the city. A good pedestrian may ride on either the Santa Fe or the "Old Town" railway from San Diego to the Old Town, or on the electric car to its terminus, then from either of these places walk to the Mission and back, but a good day is required for such a journey.

CHAPTER IV.

SAN CARLOS BORROMEO.

The next Mission to be founded was that of San Carlos Borromeo, at Monterey, on June 3, 1770.

Serra said mass, after which Governor Portala took possession of the port, in the name of God and the king.

Slowly the Indians were reached, attracted, converted, and Padre Serra's heart made glad, yet, at the same time, he felt that the close proximity of the presidio was not advantageous to his work. So, in a few months, he withdrew to the Carmelo Valley, and there, by December, 1770, a chapel was erected, also several dwellings for the priests and the neophytes, as well as corrals for the sheep and cattle. The little settlement was enclosed within a palisade.

After various difficulties, San Carlos began to prosper, and for many years it was exceedingly wealthy. The influence of the priests also had much to do with the welfare of the neighborhood.

It is of the sweet-toned bells of this Mission that Chester Gore Miller wrote in his dramatic poem on Padre Serra :—

" When deeper shadows of the night o'ertake
In silent way the early evening hour,
Then soft and low the silver bells forsake
Their quiet vigil in the mission tower :
In rhythmic measure sound the silvery notes

As o'er the peaceful valley they vibrate ;—
How tuneful sweet the holy music floats,—
While drowsy doves in sudden flight gyrate.
So in such twilights oft I take my way,
To pray at Vespers in the place where dwells
An absolution for our sins of day ;
What consolation 'neath those saintly bells ;
    And at my death I ask no greater boon,
    Than pass away as floats their sacred tune."

Bells of San Carlos Borromeo

    San Carlos has recently been restored and is now one of the greatest objects of interest to visitors in that region. Here Padre Serra labored and suffered more than in any other Mission. Monterey was especially dear to him, and here, after his long life full of zeal and earnest devotion, he passed away. His body is buried in the Monterey Mission.

CHAPTER V.

SAN ANTONIO DE PADUA.

On July 14, 1771, San Antonio de Padua, the third Mission, was established.

Serra had long waited, impatiently, for the arrival of fresh supplies from Mexico, and, when, on the 21st of May, 1771, the *San Antonio* appeared in the bay of Monterey, his heart rejoiced, for now he could push forward the founding of the Missions he had in mind.

Accordingly, early in July, accompanied by Padres Pieras and Sitjar and a few neophytes and the necessary guard of soldiers and provisions, he set out from San Carlos. The party "traveled southward till they reached a beautiful dell, which on account of its being thickly covered with oak trees, they called 'Los Robles.' Here they halted, carefully surveyed the place and found a plain skirting the bank of a river; this spot they selected as the most suitable location for the Mission, which they named San Antonio. Though in midsummer, they noticed that the river had a plentiful flow of water, hence they concluded that in time the land around could be irrigated."

The mules were unloaded, the bell suspended from a branch of a tree, and Padre Serra immediately began to ring it, crying aloud: "Oh Indians, come, come, come to the Holy Church; come, come to receive the faith of Jesus Christ!"

On being remonstrated with by Padre Miguel Peiras, Serra replied, "Ah! let me satisfy the longing of my own heart. Would to God the voice of this

San Antonio de Padua

bell could resound through the whole world, as Mother Agreda desired. I wish it could be heard by all the Indians who inhabit these mountains."

A large cross was made, blessed, venerated and erected, a hut covered with boughs built, a table placed for the altar and on the 14th of July, the first mass was celebrated by Serra in honor of Saint Anthony, the patron of the Mission.

Under the wise direction of the padres it grew and prospered. In two years there were one hundred and fifty-eight Christians, and at Serra's death, the number had increased to one thousand and eighty-eight.

San Antonio is situated in the center of the Sierra of Santa Lucia, separated from the sea by rugged mountains. It now stands alone. The Indians of a century ago have disappeared Once or twice a month it is visited by a priest from San Miguel.

CHAPTER VI.

SAN GABRIEL ARCHANGEL

Two months later, viz., on September 8, 1771, San Gabriel Archangel was founded. Padres Benito Cambon and Angel Somero were of the new band of missionaries who had been sent on from Mexico to aid Padre Serra, and they left San Diego August 6, 1771, accompanied by ten soldiers and muleteers, to found a mission which they intended to dedicate to their patron Saint, San Gabriel the Archangel. For days they moved slowly through a country densely covered with cactus, until they reached the banks of the Santa Ana river, where, it had been determined by the Governor, when the first expedition passed through the region,

San Gabriel Archangel

a mission should be established. After a careful search, and the fathers finding no suitable site, they moved further north and west to the San Miguel River, now known as the San Gabriel, and there founded the Mission. The original site is still marked by a few adobe ruins, and can be reached by driving from Los Angeles, or, better still, Whittier or Rivera. The location at that time was known as the Indian village of Sibanga. About the year 1775, the erection of the present building was begun and the old Mission deserted. It was fully twenty-five years before it was completed, together with the commodious residence of the Padres, and then more than 4,000 Indian neophytes had been baptized. The first baptism of an Indian child was on November 27, 1771. In two years the number of converts was 73, and in 1784 there were 1,019 enrolled on the baptismal register.

Here in 1806, came from San Fernando, Padre Jose Maria Zalvidea, under whose wise and skilful management the mission rapidly grew into great prosperity and wealth. This was the Padre, whose name "H. H.," the writer of "Ramona" incorrectly caught, and, spelling it Salvierderra, made him her priestly hero.

The building is a quaint old structure, without much architectural pretension, with a peculiar "bell tower," in which four bells are now hung, one of them not being as perfect as in "days of yore." The Padre's house is a cozy little cottage to the left of the Mission, as one stands facing it, and is beautifully embowered in sweet flowers.

San Gabriel is the oldest mission building now existing in a reasonable state of preservation, and is of added interest on this account.

The visitor should not fail to observe the extensive cactus hedges,—the remains of which still exist,— undoubtedly surrounding the mission as an additional means of protection from the incursions of wild beasts or wilder men. There are also to be seen the remains of the stone and cement aqueduct through which was conveyed water for irrigation, and for motive power to operate the old flour mills built by the padres.

One of these mill buildings still exists in a fair state of preservation, on the grounds of Col. Mayberry, a few miles from the Mission. The drive is interesting and well repays the curious visitor.

The following exquisite lines from the February, 1895, *Overland Monthly*, by L. Worthington Green, will speak of the site of the Mission, the cactus hedge, and the mission bell:

> "Franciscan Fathers deemed the spot so fair
>   They planted olives and the purple grape,
> And gentle, pastoral Indians gathered there
>   To hear the lessons planned their souls to shape.
> The circling hedge of sharp-spined prickly pear
>   Was barrier sure to all designing foe,
> But any friend who wished might enter there
>   The willing hosts' sweet charity to know.
>
> The full-voiced chime that pealed the matin call
>   And bade the toiler to the vesper chant
> Still hangs in arches of the ancient wall.
>   But now its rhythmic tones are sadly scant,
> There spaces are like empty cloister cells,
>   That echoed once the hallowed sound of bells."

One of the missing bells is now on the Santa Anita ranch—"Lucky" Baldwin's—and is hung under a little shelter near his house. It is now used to call the residents of the place to meals.

San Gabriel still has a fairly large population of Mexicans, consequently, and for the religious benefit of the old California families who are of that ancient faith, the Church is kept in a good state of repair, and regular service conducted therein.

San Gabriel is reached in a variety of ways. One may easily drive from Los Angeles or Pasadena and take in a number of other interesting historical scenes

on the way. The Southern Pacific R. R.,—the main line from Los Angeles to Yuma,—passes the old Mission, and the ancient structure is but a few minutes' walk from the depot. The distance from Los Angeles is 9 miles, the fare, single trip, 30 cents; round trip, 55 cents, and a little over half a day will suffice for the journey and return.

CHAPTER VII.

SAN LUIS OBISPO DE TOLOSA.

Just one year later (less one week), after the founding of San Gabriel Archangel, viz., on September 1, 1772, Padre Serra, with Padre Cavaller, five soldiers and a few of his San Carlos Indians, who had left Monterey some days previously, established the Mission of San Luis Obispo de Tolosa, on a site called by the Indians "Tixlini," near the Canyada de Los Osos, (The Valley of the Bears). The land in the neighborhood was arable, and a creek with plenty of water flowed near by. As usual, Serra erected a cross, sang Mass, invited the Indians to come and be converted, and at the conclusion of the ceremony the Mission was founded. Padre Cavaller, "with the Indians from Lower California and four soldiers with their corporal," at once set to work to erect a building, Padre Serra having left for San Diego the day after the foundation. Soon, a chapel, a house for the Padre, and barracks for the soldiers were finished, and, with their native curiosity aroused, the Indians speedily began to flock to the scene. The Padre worked wisely and well; and when Padre Palou visited the Mission the following year, he found twelve persons baptized

San Isidro, Obispo de Palos

in the faith. The soldiers made friends with the Indians, even the unconverted ones, and the result was that venison, seeds and bear's meat constantly found their way into the larder of the priest and soldiers through the kindness of the simple-hearted natives.

There is no doubt that much of the friendly feeling on the part of the natives was owing to the fact that the year previous, during the food famine at the Monterey mission, Commandant Fages had hunted and slain a large number of bear in the region of the new mission of San Luis Obispo de Tolosa. The Indians, thankful that the dreaded bears were slain, naturally received their slayers with much warmer cordiality than they would otherwise have been apt to accord to strangers.

After the first year of arduous labor and weary toil, San Luis Obispo saw better days. Padre Juncosa joined Padre Cavaller, supplies were forwarded from the common stores at San Diego and Monterey, and the foundations were laid for the successful career that this mission enjoyed until the direful hand of secularization smote it to despair and death.

Speaking of the Indians who were "converted" by the Padre, or subjugated to the lash of the soldiers, one writer says: " Serra found them utter barbarians, naked, living on seeds, roots, and all kinds of flesh they could procure with bows and arrows, and when hard pushed for food, eating any living thing, down to snakes and crickets. Brave they could not have been; but sometimes fierce and tumultuous. Morality, as understood in the civilized world, was unknown to them ; and they were at least as superstitious as those who came to teach them."

It is to the disasters that befell the earliest mission buildings of San Luis Obispo that we are indebted for the picturesque brick tiles that protect several of the remaining ruined mission buildings. Three times was the mission building at this place burned down, and

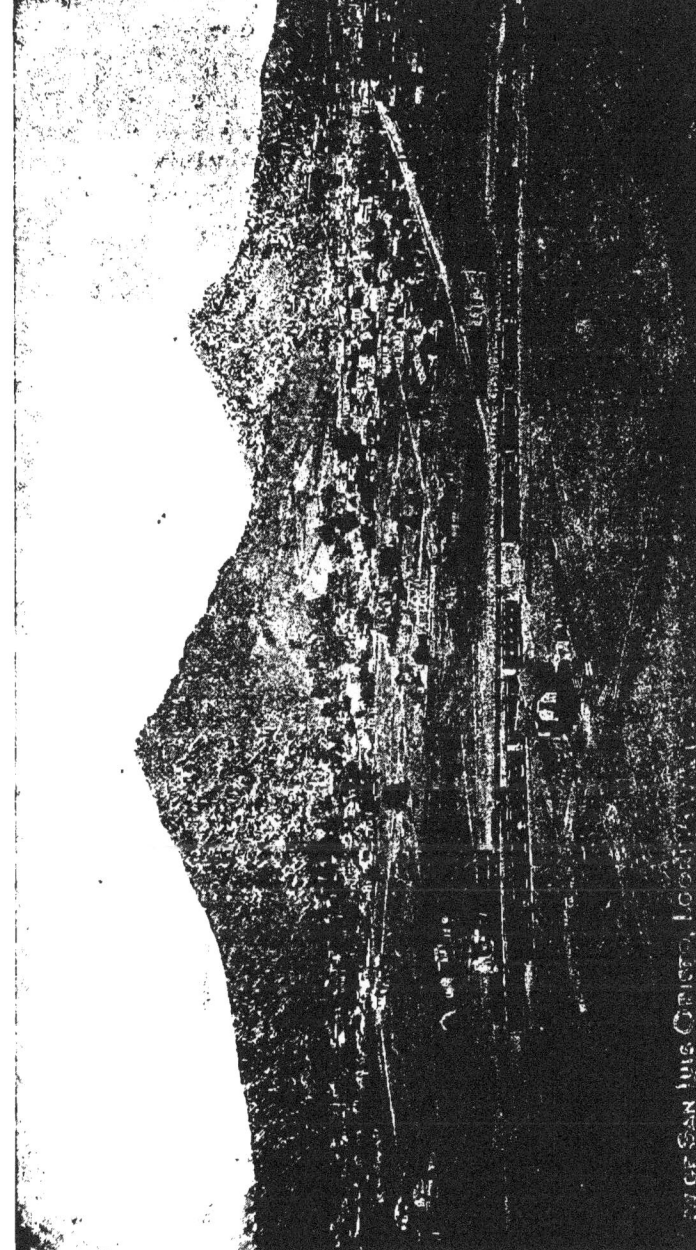

this series of misfortunes led one of the padres to attempt—successfully, as it proved—the making of roof tiles, which took the place of the inflammable tules and willows. What a pity it is the name of the "tile-making padre" has not come down to us that we might canonize him for his work.

To the sailors and traders along the coast early in the century, few figures were better known and better liked than that of the picturesque Padre Luis Martinez of San Luis Obispo. "Portly of figure and gruff of speech" he was jolly, hale-fellow-well-met, hospitable, and, if reports and suspicions count for anything, always ready to trade for his own advantage. Anyhow, in the spring of 1830, on this same charge he was banished, and, with many tears and much regret, he was compelled to say farewell to the mission he so much loved, and the Indians he had sought to benefit, to return in disgrace to old Madrid, where he spent the remainder of his days.

H. H., in Ramona, in describing the wedding tour and festivities of General and Senora Moreno, tells a good story which perfectly illustrates the jolly character of Padre Martinez. She says: "On the morning of their departure, the good padre, having exhausted all his resources for entertaining his distinguished guests, caused to be driven past the corridors for their inspection, all the poultry belonging to the Mission. The procession took an hour to pass. For music there was squeaking, cackling, hissing, gobbling, crowing, and quacking of the fowls, combined with the screaming, scolding, and whip cracking of the excited Indian marshals of the lines. First came the turkeys, then the roosters, then the white hens, then the black, and then the yellow; next the ducks, and at the tail of the spectacle long files of geese, some struggling, some half flying and hissing in resentment and terror at the unwonted coercion to which they were subjected. The Indians had been hard at work all night capturing, sorting, assorting, and guarding the rank and file of their novel pageant. It would be safe to say that a droller sight never was seen, and never will be, on the Pacific coast or any other. Before it was done with, the General and his bride had nearly died with

San Luis Obispo Entrance

laughter; and the General could never allude to it without laughing almost as heartily again."

The earthquake of 1812, which caused much disturbance, somewhat affected this Mission, but, in its ruined condition, it still remains, a silent, deserted memorial to its former greatness.

It is easily reached now by rail from San Francisco, or by rail from Los Angeles to Santa Barbara and thence by stage, and, doubtless, within a comparatively short time, the Southern Pacific Railroad,—which is rapidly pushing its coast division so as to afford an entirely different route from the one now followed in going from Los Angeles to San Francisco,—will have united its present termini, thus bringing San Luis Obispo within a few hours' reach of Los Angeles, as was Padre Serra's original intention when the Mission was founded.

CHAPTER VIII.

SAN FRANCISCO DE ASIS.

Four years and sixteen days elapsed after the founding of San Luis Obispo, and then the Mission of San Francisco de Asis, on Oct. 9, 1776, was formally dedicated. This Mission is often referred to as the "Mission Dolores." It is simply the Mission of San Francisco de Asis on the River Dolores.

General M. G. Vallejo, in an oration delivered by him at the Centennial Commemoration of the San Francisco Mission states that "the temporary building of the church was situated at a distance of about one thousand varas to the northwest of the spot where the actual temple now stands. The lake of Dolores was at the time located and could be seen to the right of the road coming from the Presidio to the Mission between two hills, one of which still exists, the other one has disappeared before the progressive march of this rich emporium."

The captain of the packet-boat left four of his men to aid in building the Mission, and in 1781, when Padre Serra visited San Francisco for the first time he had the great joy of administering the rite of confirmation to sixty-nine neophytes.

From General Vallejo I quote the following: "When they had a pretty large congregation of converts under subjection, they dedicated them to works of industry. Besides the agricultural pursuits, from which the missionaries as well as the neophytes and catechumens were to receive their subsistence, adobes, bricks, tiles, etc., were made, and the construction of the holy temple was begun; granaries, residence, quarters and a guard house for the soldiers, and lastly houses for the Indians who had been converted to Christianity, were built. It will be readily seen by this account that the most worthy Fathers were constantly employed in their spiritual as well as temporal labors; although the latter were always subordinate to the former.

"In one of my journeys to San Francisco, during the year 1826, I found this Mission in all its splendor and state of preservation, consisting, at that time, of one church, the residence of the Reverend Father, granaries, warehouses for merchandise, guard-house for the soldiers, prison, an orchard of fruit trees and vegetable garden, cemetery, the entire rancheria (Indian village), all constructed of adobe houses with tile roofs, the whole laid out with great regularity, forming streets, and a tannery and soap factory—that is to say, on that portion which actually lies between Church, Dolores and Guerrero streets, from north to south, and between Fifteenth and Seventeenth streets from east to west. I think that the neophytes living in the Mission, in San Mateo, and in San Pedro reached six hundred souls."

What a change in a hundred years. Indians in large numbers, wild, barren, uncultivated country, a harbor in which a vessel was seldom seen, the building of a presidio and a mission by a handful of strangers who felt themselves indeed "in a strange and far-off country." Now the flags of all nations float in the harbor, around which populous cities have sprung up. The electric light has taken the place of the Indians' rude torches, the cable and electric cars, of the wild ponies upon which they dashed to and fro. The Indians have totally disappeared, and the only object that links the "now" with the "then" is the old Mission Dolores, a true memorial of "deeds heroic-

A Primitive Indian Residence

ally bold," and of the power of the cross to send timid men into the midst of unknown dangers.

In 1833, William Heath Davis says he paid a visit to the Mission Dolores, and he there saw gathered from 2000 to 2500 Indians. The order and discipline among them was so good as to excite the admiration of all who beheld them. He says: "It seemed like a military camp. The men dressed in white shirts and blue drill or cotton pants; many of them with shoes, which were manufactured at the Missions, from bullock hides, deer or elk skins, tanned and dressed there.

The government of the Indians was systematic and well designed. A few of the Indians, in whom the Padres had confidence, were selected to act as alcades or capitanes, each over a certain number, for whose good conduct he was in some degree responsible. If any offence against the regulations of the Mission

Using the Metate

was committed, the case was reported to the Padre, who determined what punishment should be inflicted on the culprit."

CHAPTER IX.

SAN JUAN CAPISTRANO.

A month later, Nov. 1, 1776, San Juan Capistrano was founded by President Serra, aided by Padres Mugartegui and Amurrio. In the preceding year Padres Lasuen and Amurrio with a few soldiers were sent out from Monterey to seek a location for the establishment of a new Mission, to bear the name of San Juan Capistrano. Padre Amurrio remained at

Bells and Ruined Church of San Juan Capistrano

San Gabriel, his coadjutor going on alone, and on October 30th, he found a desirable spot, where a cross was erected, a hut built of boughs of trees, and Mass celebrated. The Indians were friendly, aiding the new comers in the cutting down of timber for the building, and matters progressed happily. Eight days later Padre Amurrio arrived with provisions, etc., from San Gabriel, and all were filled with joy at the happy inauguration of the new endeavor. That evening, however, terrible news were received by messenger from San Diego. The Indians had revolted, slain Padre Jayme, and destroyed the Mission buildings. The officer in charge of the soldiers left immediately for San Diego. The Padres buried the bells, and taking the other material they had with them along, speedily followed the soldiers. What they found at San Diego has already been recounted.

This terrible affair delayed the founding of San Juan Capistrano for about a year. The Viceroy wrote from Mexico, April 3, 1776, that he had given orders to his officers to establish the Mission. Captain Rivera, who, for some reason seemed to oppose the establishment of the new Mission, was ordered, in a subsequent letter, to give Padre Serra the help he needed, so he detailed ten of the military, and with these, and accompanied by Padres Mugartegui and Amurrio "he proceeded to the place where the bells had been buried, and with the usual ceremonies founded the Mission of San Juan Capistrano."

Serra with the aid of an interpreter, explained to the Indians the purpose of the priests in coming amongst them, and we are told that, "while the Indians of the other Missions were, in the beginning, over-anxious for bodily comforts, those of San Juan were solicitous only for baptism, asking it most earnestly from the Missionaries, and finding the time required for preliminary instruction too long."

When Padre Serra died there were 470 Indian

Christians at the Mission ; and the number afterwards increased so rapidly that in three months the Missionaries baptized more than they had received before in the past three and a half years.

The earthquake of 1812, that practically shattered San Luis Obispo, visited dire destruction upon the buildings of San Juan Capistrano, as well as left its ruins full of tragic memories. It was on the morning of Dec. 8th, that the catastrophe happened.

An adobe apartment close by the Church, fortunately escaped the general destruction, and in this building the Indians for many days after the earthquake assembled, and the Mexicans and Whites of to-day, assemble and worship on the Sabbath and special feast days. There is no resident priest, however, services now being conducted by the Rev. Father O'Keefe of San Luis Rey, formerly so well known at Santa Barbara.

It is difficult as one now stands amid the bewilderment of ruined buildings, corridors and houses to repeople the place with the scores of Indians who once made this their happy home, and yet, where desolation now reigns supreme, there were once, a few generations ago, a busy and active people engaged in the varied labors outlined in a preceding page.

Look at its ruins now. Sadness and desolation have fallen over the scene. The majestic towers are gone, the ruined corridors and arches alone remain to tell the story of the many Indians who once made this their home. Melrose Abbey is not more interesting, and in surroundings, especially in the rainy season, is not so beautiful, even though "seen by the pale moonlight." Standing on the high ground by the Mission, the view is perfect. Encircled by green hills, a lovely green valley reaches out to the placid face of the ocean on whose bosom ships lazily glide to and fro. No wonder the site attracted the attention of the observant padre, and it is scarcely to be wondered

In the Ruined Corridors of San Juan Capistrano

at, either, that it was one of the most populous of all the Missions.

San Juan Capistrano is the Mission of patriotic recollections. The same year upon which the famous "Declaration of Independence" was being forced upon the attention of the world, on the Atlantic side, saw the founding of this building. It was originally built almost entirely of stone and mortar, and in one place was successfully solved one of the most difficult of architectural problems,—the triple arch. Guided by the padres the Indians were the builders of this beautiful structure. As one writer well says: "A semi-savage origin is traceable in all one sees. The long rows of arches are stately only after a barbaric fashion, wonderful as they are for the time and circumstances of their construction, and picturesque because proclaiming Spain in miniature, and coming by a wonderfully long road from Palestine itself. But they are not precisely alike. The hand of the Indian is visible in their curves. Some are longer than their fellows by a finger's breadth, and some are slightly higher in the bend. Among the red tiles of the pillars some are thick and some are thin. Symmetry, either of material or architecture, is not to be expected of the savage of any race, and for all the purposes of picturesque decay the result answers quite as well."

The above statement is true, and I have quoted it because few people are observant enough to notice the fact, without first having their attention called to it, and yet, the variations in measurement are so slight as to require careful observation to detect.

There are a number of traditions rife, here and there, about San Juan Capistrano Mission. One is to the effect that Bonsard, a noted pirate, with his followers, once occupied it for three days in a great debauch, while the priest and neophytes,—except those unfortunate ones who were kept to minister to the evil passions of these lawless men,—were banished

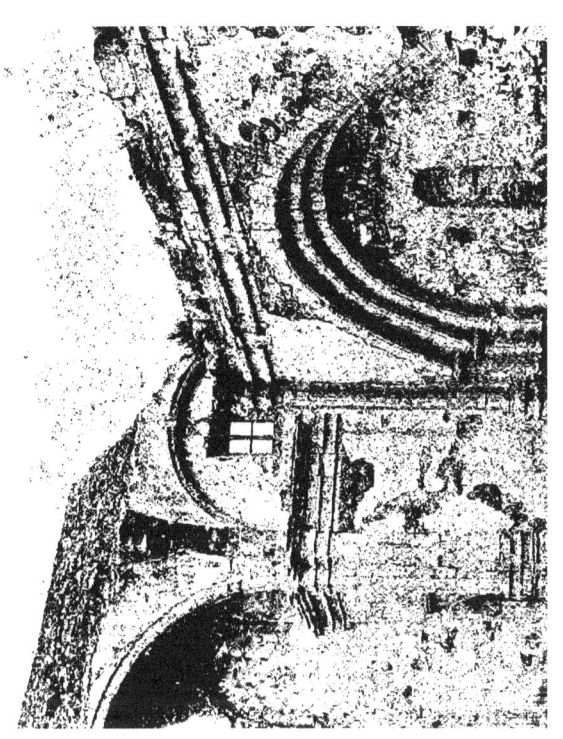

to Trabuco Creek until the revelers had departed. In 1833 Capistrano suffered with the other missions from the dread order of secularization. The herds were soon scattered or slain, everything that could be converted into money was sold, the books of the old library scattered, and even the records of the church, some of them, taken away or carelessly destroyed. Those of the Indians who were deemed sufficiently civilized, were allotted lands, and were no longer regarded as under the domination of the padres, though spiritually, of course, they still came to the fathers for guidance.

When Micheltorena came from Mexico, in 1842, to take control of California as its governor, he landed in San Diego, where a great reception was given him, and then he came in a kind of triumphal procession northward. At San Juan Capistrano a feast of two or three days' duration was held, and then, doubtless, he learned for himself the sad condition of the mission Indians and the buildings. The following year he ordered San Juan to be restored to the padres, but it was too late to stay the demoralization of either the buildings or the Indians. The land could not be recovered, although a few of the mission herds were traced and brought back. The revolution which banished Micheltorena, a year later, however, brought a new order, which was for the sale of the Mission, and it was purchased by James McKinley and John Foster for the sum of seven hundred and ten dollars. For twenty years Foster held undisputed possession, when the Catholic Church claimed the buildings and immediately surrounding premises. In court the claim of the church was allowed, and these picturesque ruins are now under its absolute control.

San Juan Capistrano received its name from Portala, the first Governor of California. As he journeyed from San Diego to Monterey, where he came to this place, which he says was a "lovely valley," they

found the Indians, naked, but painted in different colors, so friendly as to come out and meet them with simple and unaffected cordiality. The women were modestly covered. The painting of their bodies was a sign of great respect, and they met Portala with marked ceremony, the chief making a speech, at the close of which all the Indians "let their arms drop to the ground." After exchanging presents with the Indians, Portala named the place San Juan Capistrano, which name it still retains, and undoubtedly ever will.

The tourist, who imagines he can see San Juan Capistrano Mission, or any other, by merely riding by on the cars, is much mistaken, and many lose the enjoyment they might have, by so doing. At Capistrano this is not necessary, for experience has taught me where I might stay and find most comfortable quarters and excellent board. Mr. and Mrs. Mendelson, who own the village store, etc., seeing the large number of people who desired to enjoy the Mission, but who knew not where they might stay, built a home-like hotel, where they now make comfortable those to whom the old Mission has proven a sufficient allurement. Mrs. Mendelson is thoroughly well posted on all the main objects of interest, and kindly escorts the tourist to the building, points out all he desires to see, introduces him to the sacristan, and this renders the visit most interesting and profitable. Her bedrooms are comfortable, neat and scrupulously clean, and her table wholesome, tasty and appetizing.

In the store Mr. Mendelson will show you samples of the walnuts, etc., grown in the region. Capistrano is as good nut and fruit growing a country as is to be found in South California, and he is always proud to show what the soil of the old padre's choice can still produce.

One can well spend a week at Capistrano. The hot springs are both an attraction, and, to those who use them, a benefit, and the trip to the beach, and San Juan Point is interesting both to sight-seers and to those who have read Dana's accounts of how they used to load hides from the old Mission. Mr. Mendelson furnishes conveyances to those who wish to visit either of these places.

San Juan Capistrano is 59 miles distant from Los Angeles, and is reached on the Surf Line of the Santa Fe route. The single fare is $1.90, round trip $3.40. On Sundays only, returning the same day, a special rate of $1.50 is given, and going on Saturday, returning Monday, the round trip is $2. Fair hotel accommodations are provided for those who desire to stay over night. Those who wish to make a hasty visit can arrange to go down from Los Angeles on their way to San Diego, on the morning train, obtain a stop-over, visit the Mission, and then proceed on the evening train.

CHAPTER X.

SANTA CLARA.

Santa Clara was the next Mission founded, in the year 1777, by Padre Tomas de la Peña, at the head of the broad fertile valley of San Bernardino near San Jose, in Santa Clara County.

On the 6th of January, 1777, a party of armed soldiers, under the command of Lieutenant Moraga, with an escort, and Father Tomas, went to the chosen spot, and another party came later, accompanying Padre Jose Murguia, from San Carlos, bringing provisions and supplies for the new mission. Both priests were to remain in charge of the new establishment, but as Padre Murguia did not arrive until the 21st, Padre Pena celebrated mass and founded the mission in honor of the pious maiden of Assisi, on the 12th.

At the end of the first year these two toilers had

baptized sixty-seven Indians into the fold, besides receiving fourteen others, who, as they were dying, desired the offices of the church.

Although the spot chosen was exceedingly fertile, it was in constant danger in the winter time from freshets in the river caused by the heavy rains and melting snow, and in 1779, the anticipated danger became real, for the mission and its surroundings were flooded, several houses floated off their foundation and considerable damage was effected.

This led to the removal of the buildings to higher ground, the spot upon which the present ruins now stand, and, on the 15th of May, 1784, Padre Serra was present at the dedication of the new church, assisted by Padres Pena and Palou. We are told that it was the most beautiful and elaborate that up to that time had been erected. Its architect was Padre Murguia, but, alas! as is so often the case with arduous toilers towards a desired object, just as it was completed he passed away four days before the dedication, and was buried beneath its walls.

This structure was shaken by a heavy earthquake in 1818, which led to the building of a new mission in 1825-6, and it is the ruins of this latest structure that the interested tourist sees.

Santa Clara Mission has been the scene of most exciting and interesting events. Davis tells of a young man named Yoscolo, who was trained at Santa Clara by the padres, and who, at the age of twenty-one, was made chief of the Indians of that neighborhood, responsible, as I have before explained, to the padres for his management of them. He was evidently a born leader, for, when some of his tribe committed depredations for which the padres proposed to punish him, he refused to submit, and, at once, revolted with 500 of his charge.

Armed with bows and arrows they broke open the mission stores and helped themselves to blankets and whatever articles they desired, and could easily carry away. Then, fired by their successes they broke into the convent where the Indian girls were, and reversed the padres' method of mating, which consisted of letting the girls choose from a batch of young fellows, who were brought into their presence. They seized upon 200 of the maidens, who, to tell the truth, were doubtless not unwilling to be captured, and then, driving about two thousand head of horses before them they escaped to the mountains above Mariposa. This occurred in 1831.

Another Indian, Stanislaus by name, and from whom Stanislaus river and county were named, had also revolted from the mission of San Jose, and was at the head of about 4,000 Indians* at Mariposa. Yoscolo joined Stanislaus, and became fast friends, the latter placing Yoscolo at the head of their united forces.

General Vallejo immediately organized a force of 200 men and set off in pursuit of the renegades, but, by a wily trick, the Californians were put off the scent and the aborigines escaped. In the light of the moon the Indians sent a number of large bundles of grass afloat down the stream, and these, passing by Vallejo's camp, his soldiers mistook them for Indians and set off after them in hot pursuit. It was a long time before they discovered their error, and in the meantime Yoscolo and his forces had retreated to some well-nigh inaccessible mountain recesses where he knew he would be free from exterior disturbance.

A little later, Yoscolo, with about 200 picked men, made another raid on the mission, plundering the stores and carrying off a large amount of valuable goods to a retreat he had found in the Santa Cruz mountains, near to where Los Gatos now stands.

This aroused the Californians to a determined course of conduct, and, Juan Prado Mesa, the military

---
*Davis says 40,000. I think this is an error and should be 4,000.

commander of Santa Clara Mission, organized a force with which he went out to meet the renegade. Not having a large band, and the soldiers being men whom he knew, Yoscolo was emboldened to come part of the way down the mountain to meet his pursuers. A fierce encounter ensued. Yoscolo "marshalled his forces in the form of a square, in true military style, and ordered his men to lie down and discharge their arrows from a recumbent position, in which there would be less risk of being hit by the bullets of their opponents, who were armed with the old-fashioned muskets, carbines and flint-lock pistols. The battle raged all day, the savages showing great stubbornness in continuing it. Only when all their arrows had been discharged did they finally yield to the Californians. Their leader, when taken, was found to be wounded. He and the more prominent of the band under him were immediately beheaded. The remainder were turned over to the mission of Santa Clara to be civilized and christianized anew. About one hundred Indians were killed and wounded in the battle. Of the Californians only eight or ten were killed, but a large number were wounded.

Yoscolo's head was fixed to the top of a pole planted in front of the church at Santa Clara, and remained there for several days as a warning to other Indians.

In 1839, Don Jose Ramon Estrada, the duly appointed *comisionado*, gave away or sold the fertile mission lands to his friends and supporters, and the mission consequently soon fell into decay. The Indians protested, but their unsupported efforts amounted to nothing. From that day to this the work of decay has gone on, and now not an Indian remains, the buildings are in sad ruins, only an adobe chapel and a few lands in the possession of the Jesuits are left to tell of a glory departed and forever lost.

CHAPTER XI.

SAN BUENAVENTURA.

From the very inception of the Upper California Mission project Serra had always determined that a Mission should be dedicated to San Buenaventura, and that it should be located somewhere about midway between San Diego and Monterey. Again and again had he urged its founding, and each time some obstacle intervened to prevent. Political changes had also taken place that were not advantageous to the plans of the good Padre. The Viceroy Bucareli, who had been his good friend, died, and henceforth, Serra was to have to deal with a Captain-General of the Californians, instead of directly with the Viceroy. In June, 1779, he received the information that his majesty—the King of Spain—had taken away California from the jurisdiction of the new Viceroy, and appointed Don Teodore de Croix, Captain-General, and that he would reside in Sonona. Don Felipe de Neve was the new Governor, who had taken Portala's place, so Serra had now three officials to deal with. Many annoyances were the result of this new arrangement, but, with persistent energy, Serra kept diligently working towards the high and holy end he had in view. Letter after letter were sent to the new Viceroy, and the result was the latter sent a letter to Captain-General de Croix, which had such an effect upon him that he ordered Rivera "to recruit seventy-five soldiers for the establishment of a presidio and three Missions in the Channel of Santa Barbara. One towards the north of the Channel, which was to be

San Buenaventura Mission

dedicated to the Immaculate Conception ; one towards the south, dedicated to San Buenaventura, and a third in the center, dedicated to Santa Barbara."

It was Serra's intense desire that the whole of the Indians along the two hundred leagues of Pacific Coast should be converted, and he argued that if Missions were established at convenient intervals of dis tance, they would be caught in one or the other of them. Portala, after he made his trip from San Diego to Monterey, reported fully to Serra the condition of the Indians he found on the shore of the Channel Coast. How that they, by means of pictures made in the sand, showed that vessels had been there, and white men, with beards, also had visited them ; thus, undoubtedly, recalling the traditions of the Vizcaino visit made nearly two hundred years before. Portala described their huts and the arrangement of their villages. The one he named "Assumpta" was the site of the future San Buenaventura. There, he found the Indians more industrious and athletic, and the women better clad, than elsewhere. They were builders of wellshaped pine canoes, and were expert fishermen. They were also stone-masons, using only tools made of flint. Exchanges were made by Portala with them of curious trinkets for highly polished wooden plates, which showed that they were accomplished wood-workers. Each family lived in its own hut, which was conical in shape, made of willow poles and covered with sage and other brush. A hole was left in the top for the smoke to escape which rose from the fire, always built in the center of the hut.

Reports such as these had kept Serra in a constant ferment to establish the long-promised Mission there, so we can imagine it was with intense delight that he received a call from Governor Neve, who in February, 1783, informed him that he was prepared to proceed at once to the founding of the Missions of San Buenaventura and Santa Barbara. Although busy training his neophytes, he determined to go in person and perform the necessary ceremonies. Looking about for a padre to accompany him, and all his own coadjutors being engaged, he bethought him of Father Pedro Benito Cambon, a returned invalid Missionary from the Philippine Islands who was recuperating at San Diego. He accordingly wrote Padre Cambon requesting him, if possible, to meet him at San Gabriel. On his way to San Gabriel, Serra passed through the Indian villages of the Channel region, and could not refrain from joyfully communicating the news to the Indians that, very speedily, he would return to them, and establish Missions in their midst. I have often wondered, and still wonder, what the thoughts of the Indians were, as this man,—benignant, energetic, devout,—talked with them and revealed his purposes towards them. Who can tell?

In the evening of March 18, Serra reached Los Angeles, and next evening, after walking to San Gabriel, weighed down with his many cares, and weary with his long walk, he still preached an excellent sermon, it being the feast of the patriarch St. Joseph. Father Cambon had arrived, and after due consultation with him and the Governor, the date for the setting out of the expedition was fixed for Tuesday, March 26th. The week was spent in confirmation services, and other religious work, and, on the date named, after solemn mass, the party set forth. It was the most imposing procession ever witnessed in California up to that time, and called forth many gratified remarks from Serra. There were seventy soldiers, with their captain, commander for the new presidio, ensign, sergeant, and corporals. In full gubernatorial dignity, followed Governor Neve, with ten soldiers of the Monterey company, their wives and families, servants and neophytes.

At midnight they halted, and a special messenger overtook them with news which led the Governor to

San Buenaventura Mission

return at once to San Gabriel with his ten soldiers. He ordered the procession to proceed, however, found the San Buenaventura Mission, and there await his return. Serra accordingly went forward, and on the 29th inst., arrived at "Assumpta." Here, the next day, on the feast of Easter, they pitched their tents, "erected a large cross and prepared an altar under a shade of evergreens," where the venerable Serra, now soon to close his life work, blessed the cross and the place, solemnized mass, preached a sermon to the soldiers on the Resurrection of Christ, and formally dedicated the Mission to God, and placed it under the patronage of St. Joseph.

In the earlier part of this century the Mission began to grow rapidly. Padres Francisco Dumetz and Vicente de Santa Maria, who had been placed in charge of the Mission from the first, were gladdened by many accessions, and the Mission flocks and herds also increased rapidly. Indeed we are told that "in 1802, Ventura possessed finer herds of cattle and richer fields of grain than any of her contemporaries, and her gardens and orchards were visions of wealth and beauty."

As one looks at the old walls he recalls when a fierce battle raged around them. In March, 1838, the opposing forces of Carrillo and Alvarado met here, and Laura Bride Powers in her "Story of the Old Missions of California," graphically states that "during the bombardment a rifleman stationed in the church tower fired a deadly shot into the ranks of the enemy, felling a leader; forthwith the guns of the opposing forces bore down upon the church, the shot and shell beating against the walls with dogged determination. The din of battle over and the smoke uplifted, the chapel was found to have stood invincible. The heavy guns, however, left their marks upon the whitewashed walls in seams and scars, though time, ere this, has almost healed the wounds of battle."

Altar at San Buenaventura Mission

Father Rubio, an accomplished linguist, an excellent priest and a good man, is now in charge of San Buenaventura church. Out of veneration for his exalted character Professor T. S. C. Lowe has retained the name "Rubio" for the canyon reached by the electric-trolley portion of his wonderful mountain railway. In 1892, anxious to restore the church to, at least, a suitable condition for worship, he raised the necessary funds and in 1893 the renovating work was commenced.

"The walls of the old Mission, which used to be the color of the adobe,—the material they are made of, —are now frescoed in water colors. The columns and wainscoting resemble grey marble and granite, and there is painted on the spaces between the columns, high up on the walls, trailing vines and other artistic ornaments. Around the top of the walls and next the ceiling is a band representing carved brown wood. A number of religious emblems can be seen on the walls above the confessionals. The steps leading up to the sanctuary are made to imitate grey granite and the ones directly in front of the altar are of red granite. The sanctuary floor is an exact imitation of inlaid work, in the center of which is a double star of grey marble."

Some of the hands and other portions of the statuary had been damaged in the long years of their existence, and these have been re-sculptured and regilded.

There are a few things that are not modernized. The side doors, the baptistery and the confessionals have been preserved in the same state as they were when the Mission fathers put them in their places.

The ceiling is, for the present, in the same condition as it was left some years ago after renewing it. All it lacks is to be painted to correspond with the balance of the room, which, we understand, will be done in the near future.

The church was re-blessed, in February, 1894, by

Rev. Father Adam, of Los Angeles, with very impressive ceremonies.

San Buenaventura, or Ventura, as this modern, railroad age, has rechristened it, is on the line of the S. P. R. R., between Los Angeles and Santa Barbara. The distance is 83 miles and the rate of fare, single trip, $2.50; round trip, $4.50. Special round trip tickets good for going on Saturday and returning Tuesday, $3.00. Ventura, being the county seat, has good hotels, where the visitor desiring a lengthy stay can be accommodated.

CHAPTER XII.

SANTA BARBARA.

In April of 1782, on the return of Governor Neve, a party of sixty soldiers, with their officers, set forth to establish the Presidio and Mission of Santa Barbara. When about thirty miles north of San Buenaventura, in a region thickly populated with Indians, they found a suitable place for a presidio near the beach, and where the shore "gracefully curves and forms a sort of small bay, in which they judged good anchorage would be found."

A large cross was made and erected, a booth of branches was built for a temporary chapel, containing a rude table for an altar, and then, on the 29th of April, 1782, the Governor and soldiers assisting, Padre Serra celebrated Mass, preached a sermon, after which Governor Neve took possession of the place in the name of God and the King of Spain.

On the following day they began the erection of a chapel, barracks for the soldiers and a storehouse, Serra directing much of the work and giving spiritual instructions to the soldiers at the same time. He waited a few days, expecting the Mission would be

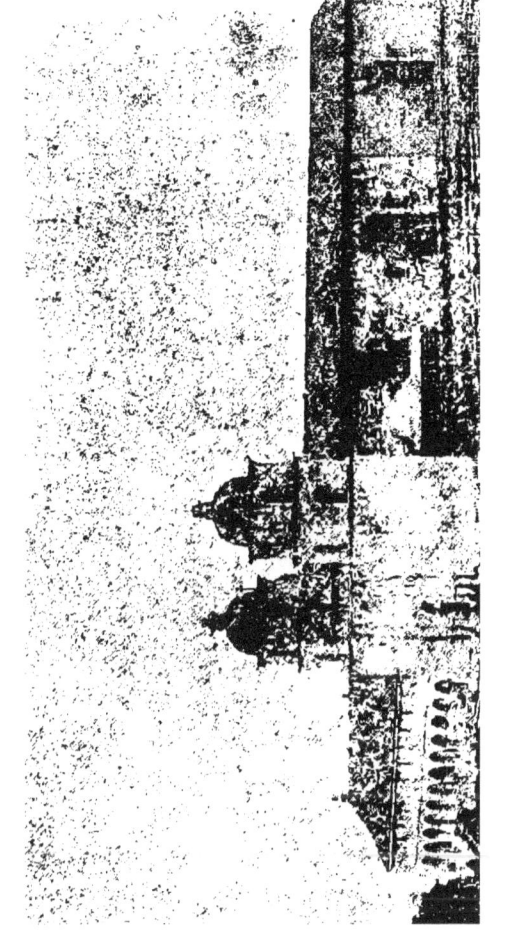

immediately founded, but in this he was disappointed. The Governor decided that, for the safety of all concerned, in a place where there were so many Indians, it was essential that the presidio be finished first, so, after sending for a priest from San Juan Capistrano, he departed for Monterey, on foot, as usual. Only once again did he see Santa Barbara, and the Mission was not yet founded, and full of sadness he cried out in bitter tears: "Pray ye, therefore, the Lord of the Harvest, that He send laborers into His vineyard." The good padre died on the 28th of August, 1784, a little before 2 o'clock, p. m., in the seventieth year of his age.

Father Palou, the intimate friend and biographer of Serra, was now appointed President of the Missions, but it was not until the 15th of December, 1786, when Padre Fermin Francisco de Lasuen had succeeded him that the Santa Barbara Mission was founded. Governor Pedro Fages had taken the place of Governor Neve,and he, together with a few soldiers, on the date named, accompanied Padre Lasuen to a spot already chosen, about a mile from the presidio and named by the natives "Taynayam," and the Spaniards "El Pedragoso," and there, with appropriate ceremonies, established the Mission. Padres Antonio Paterna and Cristobal Oramas were left in charge, but, owing to a severe rainy season, no buildings were erected until spring of the following year, the priests being sheltered during the meantime in the presidio.

Several buildings were then put up,—a house for the padres, a kitchen, a servants' room, a granary, and a house for the unmarried women, and also the first small chapel. These were all built of adobe, nearly three feet thick, with roofs of heavy rafters, across which long poles or canes were tied, covered with soft adobe and then thatched with straw. At the end of this year 183 Indians were converted and had connected themselves with the Mission.

The following year, 1788, these buildings were all tiled, others erected, and the reports show the Indians increased to 307.

In 1789, the second church of the Mission was erected, together with other needed buildings. In 1793 was begun the erection, finished in 1794, of a large adobe church, containing six chapels.

In 1806, a reservoir of stone and mortar was built for storing water for the gardens and orchards. It is still in good condition and is part of the system of the water company which now supplies the city with water.

The following year the padres built a strong dam across the " Pedragoso " creek, about a mile and a half above the Mission, from whence the water could flow in an open aqueduct to the mill reservoir. This mill and reservoir were built at the same time, behind the one referred to, and is still in use. The mill is in ruins, and the reservoir partially demolished, but it could easily be repaired and made to do good service.

In 1813-14 the old church was taken down, and a new stone church commenced in 1815. Five years later, viz., on the 10th day of September, 1820, it was completed, and amid the greatest rejoicing and festivities ever indulged in, in the country, it was formally dedicated and opened.

Owing to its prosperity, Santa Barbara was always heavily taxed by the Government, even when under the rule of Spain, but when Mexico declared its independence, it was plundered on all sides. Money being scarce in those days, as now, a large amount of cattle, sheep or wool was necessary to raise a small amount of ready money. Hence when these excessive and arbitrary demands for money were made, it taxed the resources of the mission to the last degree, and often caused great suffering to the dependent Indians.

Here, as elsewhere, secularization accomplished,

somewhat, its ruinous work, although the buildings have always been in the possession of the Franciscans, except between the years 1833 and 1835, and even then they were practically under their control.

The Mission passed through various vicissitudes, until 1853, when, a petition having been presented to Rome, it was erected into an Hospice, as the beginning of what was to be an Apostolic College for the education of novitiates.

Being ecclesiastically isolated from the rest of the United States, and therefore having no means of drawing upon other communities for its novitiates, the Minister-General petitioned that it be changed from an independent college, and annexed to the order throughout the United States. The petition was granted in 1885, and it now forms an integral part of the " Province of the Sacred Heart of Jesus," whose headquarters are in the city of St. Louis, Mo.

Thus from educating Indians, the Mission of Santa Barbara has changed into a College for the education of its priests, who may be sent on Missions or to supply any house of the Order as necessity may require. So that, independent of its history, the Mission is most interesting. And when one considers that history he cannot fail to be deeply moved. As he walks in the garden, where but two women, the Princess Louise and Mrs. President Harrison, have ever been permitted to enter, he thinks of the noble workers of the past, whose bodies lie buried there. And then as "down through the perfume-laden air, upon the sunbeam's ray, like a vision of the Holy Grail, floats the white-winged dove, Heaven's emblem of purity and peace," the thought will come that "no good and true work can ever be in vain." God allows no good thing to fall, and though the Indians are scattered, through the wicked order of Secularization, He will not suffer His own purposes to be moved.

The visitor will find Santa Barbara a most interesting Mission. The resident padres are kind and obliging, and willingly afford every reasonable facility to tourists to see all objects of interest.

Santa Barbara is reached on the line of the S. P. R. R. and is five hours' journey from Los Angeles. Fare, single trip, $3.35; round trip, $6.05. Round trip special, going Saturday, good to return the following Tuesday, $3.50. Distance, 110 miles.

As soon as the now nearly completed Coast Lines of the Southern Pacific are connected, Santa Barbara can also be reached from the north by train direct, instead of by stage from the present northern terminus of the Coast Line, or on the San Joaquin Valley main line of the S. P., via Sangus.

CHAPTER XIII.

LA PURISIMA CONCEPTION.

This is the third of the Channel series of Missions so ardently desired by Padre Serra. Originally founded, December 8, 1787, on the Santa Ynez river, it was removed later to Los Berros, across the river. The building was crude and unstable, and, in 1795, it was rapidly falling into decay. Accordingly a new edifice was erected which was dedicated in 1802.

The great earthquake of 1812 destroyed the new chapel, shook down the hundred tile-roofed dwellings of the Indians, and, to add to the horrors, a flood from the river swept away much of what was left.

Padre Mariano Payeras was the priest in charge, and, undismayed, he constructed temporary residences, warehouses for the grain soon to be garnered, and corrals for the six thousand head of cattle belonging to the Mission.

Having gained permission from Mexico to again remove the site of the Mission the present stone structure was erected, and, in 1817, duly dedicated. The building is now in ruins, and was originally a plain and simple edifice, without any pretence to the grandeur of some of the other Mission structures.

Padre Payeras, with commendable zeal, prepared a catechism and a religious manual in the native language of the fifteen hundred converts to whom he ministered, and who lived, in harmony, simplicity and contented industry, in their dwellings on the bank of the river.

When Secularization came in 1835, the Purisima Mission property was valued at but sixty thousand dollars, and the number of her Indians had dwindled down to but one hundred and twenty.

Year after year things went on from bad to worse, until in 1844, Governor Pio Pico, under direction from the Departmental Assembly, with "a curious bit of half conscience-stricken, half-politic recognition of the Indians' ownership of the lands" of the Missions, posted a proclamation at La Purisima, as well as several other Missions, bidding the Indians return and take possession of their lands, otherwise they would be sold or rented. But in 1856 the U. S. Land Commission restored the buildings to the inalienable possession of the Catholic Church, to which they still belong.

La Purisima Mission may be reached by rail to Santa Barbara and thence by stage, the distance from Santa Barbara being about forty miles.

CHAPTER XIV.

SANTA CRUZ.

Santa Cruz was the next Mission, founded by Padre Lasuen, on the San Lorenzo River, on September 25, 1791.

This was the second child of the Mission of San Francisco, the first being Santa Clara. On the 22nd of September Padre Lasuen sent Alfirez Sal and Corporal Peralta, with two *escoltas*, from San Francisco to the proposed locality, and, at Santa Clara, they were joined by Padres Alonzo Salazar and Baldomero Lopez. On the 24th the party arrived at Santa Cruz where they found a hut already prepared for them by kind neophytes from Santa Clara.

The chief of the Indians, Sugert, had gathered his tribes and brought them to witness the ceremonies, warning them not to be at all alarmed at the noise made by the guns, or "chinchinabros."

The building was formally dedicated on the 10th of May, 1794, Sugert, and all his followers, being interested witnesses of the ceremony.

In 1834-5, Ignacio del Valle, was appointed *comisionado*, to put into effect the order of secularization. He took possession of property amounting to $47,000, exclusive of the church and its lands. Ten thousand dollars of this amount was divided amongst the Indians, but, where it went the rascally whites who robbed them of it can best tell. In 1839, Hartnell found the scattered few Indians of this Mission miserably poor, and with absolutely nothing to show that they had ever received one cent.

Thus this Mission and its work sank into untimely obscurity, only to be restored to notice by the fall of its walls in 1856, when a band of treasure-seekers ruthlessly polluted the ruins, digging hither and thither in a vain search for hidden treasure.

CHAPTER XV.

LA SOLEDAD.

On October 9th of the same year, a Mission dedicated to "Our Lady of Solitude" was founded, but of its history little is known. That little I glean mainly from Laura Bride Powers's interesting "Story of the Old Missions." She says: " From a letter written by Padre Lasuen, we learn that he himself selected the site of the dolorous Mission, while on his way to Santa Cruz, early in 1791. The spot was known among the Indians as " Chuttusgelis," but to the Spaniards as "Soledad." The latter name was bestowed upon it by Portala in 1769, during his famous expedition to Monterey. In September a corps of Christian Indians left San Carlos for Soledad, to prepare for the coming of Padre Lasuen. An *enramada* was constructed, a hut erected, and on October 9th he arrived with his vestments, chasubles, etc., and said mass under a tall redwood."

As one sees its solitary ruins now, so perfectly in accord with its name, question after question occurs to the mind of the thoughtful spectator. Would the padres have gone to all the wearisome trouble and expense they did, had they been able to foresee what three score years would have brought to them? I have often wondered- and still wonder, if those brave and noble hearts would have continued their work had they seen the decree of secularization hanging over their heads? If they still look down from the world of spirits upon the scene of their labors, are they able to comprehend the why and wherefore of their failure? Quien Sabe?

CHAPTER XVI.

SAN JOSE.

On Trinity Sunday, June 11, 1796, or, according to "H. H." June 11, 1797, in accordance with commands from Mexico, which declared there must be founded in California a Mission dedicated to St. Joseph, the spiritual spouse of the Holy Virgin, Padre Lasuen established this Mission and left Padres Isadoro Barcenilla and Augustin Merino as missionaries in charge.

Its site was on the romantic foothills not far from the mission of Santa Clara, which was clearly in sight. Situated where everything that was planted grew abundantly, with a full supply of water, and a valley now known throughout the world for its wonderful fertility, and where the wild grasses give rich nourishment to the stock and sheep of the Mission, what wonder that in a few years it became exceedingly wealthy.

A large amount of trapping was done by the Indians; and William Heath Davis says that, in 1844, he received from the padre in charge at San Jose, several thousands of dollars' worth of beaver and land-otter skins, which had been collected by his neophytes on the Sacramento and San Joaquin rivers.

It was at San Jose that Stanislaus was educated, before referred to as connected with Yoscolo, the renegade, of Santa Clara. In May, 1840, Stanislaus, with a force of about eighty Indians, came down from the mountains and made a raid on several ranches near San Lorenzo and captured several hundred head of horses. A day or two afterwards, one of the plundered rancheros, Guillermo Castro, with seventeen men, set off in pursuit, coming up with the thieves on the banks of the San Joaquin river. A severe battle took place, during which quite a number were killed, and, the Californians recovering their horses, returned without any further disturbance.

Perhaps had the padres exercised a little more strict discipline on Stanislaus, he would not have given them so much trouble. After the secularization, when San Jose was under the control of Don Jose Jesus Vallejo, Davis saw an Indian whipped on the bare back. When Vallejo took possession of the mission as *Comisionado*, there were 8000 head of cattle, about 3000 head of horses, 8000 to 10,000 sheep and 1500 to 1800 Christianized Indians.

San Jose at first was only a small wooden structure with a roof of woven grasses, but some time after 1800 the building was erected, the ruins of which we now see. Being so easy of access to San Francisco and the city of San Jose, these ruins have perhaps been painted more than any other of the mission buildings.

CHAPTER XVII.

SAN JUAN BAUTISTA.

In June, 1797, San Juan Bautista was founded, the present ruined church being erected in 1800.

The locality was known to the Spaniards as "San Benito," but the Indians called it "Popeloutchom." It is a wide valley of remarkable beauty, half way between Castroville and Gilroy, and is easily reached by carriage, now-a-days, from either of these places.

Padre Presidente Lasuen, aided by Padres Martiarena and Catala with the usual help of neophytes and soldiers, performed the usual ceremonies.

The first structure was of wood, closed in with willow poles and a mud roof, but, as in the case of several others, some time after the dawn of the century, the more substantial building was erected, the ruins of which remain to this day.

Of the bells of San Juan Bautista it is said that there were originally nine, composing a chime, from a treble of one hundred pounds to a bass of many tons. These bells, *it is said*, were all cast in Peru, and the tones were remarkably rich and full. Says Charles Howard Shinn, in the *Overland* for January, 1892, " Some were afterwards cast in San Francisco, but so lost sweetness and mellowness that they were considered of little or no value. Three long remained at the old Mission. One, I have heard, was stolen by a rancher, and now, fastened to a post, serves to call his hired men to meals."

CHAPTER XVIII.

SAN MIGUEL.

Two leagues west of Santa Barbara, in order to be better able to minister to the Indians, President Lasuen and Padre Sitjar selected a station on a large rancheria called "Sagshpileel," and, on July 25, 1797, with the troops from the presidio and numbers of the Indians as witnesses, established the Mission of San Miguel, "the most glorious prince of the heavenly militia."

On the day of its founding, with great delight, Padre Sitjar presented fifteen children for baptism, and this augured well for the new Mission, as, three years later, there were gathered together at San

Miguel four hundred christianized Indians, all engaged in the peaceable pursuits the Padres had taught them.

It is related that the Padres here exercised considerable force in the conversion of Guchapa, the chief of the rancherias of the region. Padre Martin, one of Sitjar's successors, was not satisfied with the small number of braves who came for conversion, so he waited on Guchapa, and requested that he send some of his Indians to the Mission to be Christianized. The proud old chief defiantly refused, when Commander de la Guerra sent a force of fourteen men and a sergeant to take the old man prisoner. This procedure had the desired effect. The chieftain promised anything and everything required if they would only set him free, which they did, retaining his only son, however, as a hostage.

In spite of this forceful method of conversion, San Miguel was never as financially prosperous as some of the others. The crops were small, and when the Padres of San Miguel were required, in 1815, to contribute supplies for the troops of Mexico, they could only send a small quantity of wool and wine.

The Mission, however, owned large bands of sheep, and the surrounding country being especially adapted to that purpose, they might have done as well as their neighbors had they confined themselves to wool-raising and weaving.

San Miguel Mission is celebrated by Ross Browne in his "Dangerous Journey."

Only one bell remains of whatever chime San Miguel originally had, and that is swung from a pine beam that caps the pillars of the porch. "It has been there for at least fifty or sixty years, but the tradition is that three bells once hung in arches close to the eaves of red tiles."

San Miguel is in San Luis Obispo County, and is reached from Santa Barbara by stage, or by rail on the Coast Division of the S. P. R. R. from San Fran-

cisco, 207 miles, fare $6. Fare from Los Angeles to Santa Barbara, $3.35 single trip; round trip, good for ten days, $6.05. Round trip special, going Saturday, good to return the following Tuesday, $3.50. From Santa Barbara take stage.

CHAPTER XIX.

SAN FERNANDO.

It was the avowed intention of Serra to establish a complete chain of Missions from San Diego to Monterey. President Lasuen agreed with the idea, and accordingly on September 8, 1797, after having located friars at San Fernando in the dwellings of the ranchero, he dedicated the Mission to San Fernando, King of Spain, according to instructions he had received from the viceroy of Mexico.

The present ruined adobe structure displaced the original building of rude wood, tules and brush, and, in 1806, was dedicated, with imposing ceremonies, to King Fernando III, of Spain, who was canonized in 1671 by Pope Clement X.

San Fernando Mission is located in a most fertile valley,—the granary of Los Angeles county, and speedily became of considerable wealth and consequent importance.

The buildings were affected by the earthquake of 1812, and thirty new beams were added to strengthen the walls. A beautiful tiled corridor, and a large fountain and basin in the courtyard were built, the ruins of which still remain in picturesque attractiveness. Under this corridor on hot days, and by the side of this fountain on cool evenings, the Padres walked and sat and planned and studied and prayed, watching the waving palms, in the distance, and enjoying the beautiful oak and alders close by. Even in its present ruined and dilapidated condition, the semi-tropical trees and the cacti give to San Fernando the appearance of "a portion of Algeria."

In 1820 the Mission was in a flourishing condition, her vineyards and grain fields being quite extensive. In 1826 an inventory shows, besides large flocks and herds, that the Padres had merchandise in their warehouse to the value of fifty thousand dollars, besides ninety thousand dollars in specie.

In 1846 the Mission was sold by Pio Pico to Eulogio Celis for fourteen thousand dollars, for the purpose of helping towards the expenses of the war with the U. S., although, at the time, the conquest of California was practically complete. The sale was confirmed, by the U. S. Land Commission, and its Mission days were ended.

It was this year that gold was first discovered in California, at San Fernando. Some Mexicans, familiar with the placer mines, were passing north from Sonora, saw the gold and began mining it at once. That year and the next it is asserted from eighty to one hundred thousand dollars in gold dust were taken from the San Fernando placers, much of it finding its way into the hands of the local merchants at Los Angeles, San Gabriel, etc. There are still places shown in the San Fernando mountains where the "secret mines" of the padres were located, but they are now utterly deserted, though gold was taken from them up to the time of the discovery at Sutter's Creek, in 1848, and later.

Today San Fernando Mission is in an utterly ruined condition. The roof of the main building has fallen in, and nothing but the rafters keep the walls also from falling.

The Mission is about 14 miles from Los Angeles and is easily reached in less than an hour from that city on the main line of the S. P. R. R., going north. The buildings are in the valley about a mile from the depot,

and the visitor can either walk or secure a conveyance in the town. Many people find it most pleasant and agreeable to drive from Los Angeles, and it is a very comfortable day's drive.

CHAPTER XX.

SAN LUIS REY DE FRANCIA.

In 1798, on the 13th day of June, President Lasuen, assisted by Padres Santiago and Peyri founded the Mission of San Luis Rey de Francia. In beauty of site, as well as magnificence of structure, it is regarded by most people as the "King" of the Mission structures of California.

Five padres, especially, in all the older history of the Missions, stand out as the well-beloved of the Indians, and these are Serra, Palou, Crespi, Salvidea, and Peyri, and to the wonderfully persuasive and gentle character of the latter, is undoubtedly owing the great success of San Luis Rey from its inception. Not only was he possessed of the qualities that endeared him to the people, but he was also full of the same zeal as Serra, and possessed of equal administrative ability. The structure he reared was completed in 1802.

It stands upon a slight hill, gently rolling upwards from the river and the valley, which is exceedingly fertile, and gave good pasturage to the flocks and herds of the Mission. These doubled about every ten years. In 1826, Peyri had received into the folds of the church two thousand, eight hundred and sixty nine Indians. "The mission owned over twenty thousand head of cattle, and nearly twenty thousand sheep. It controlled over two hundred thousand acres of land, and there were raised on its fields in one

year three thousand bushels of wheat, six thousand of barley, and ten thousand of corn.''

In 1834, after the Secularization, San Luis Rey had an Indian population of 35,000, and possessed over 24,000 cattle, 10,000 horses, and 100,000 sheep. It harvested 14,000 fanegas (about an English bushel) of grain, and 200 barrels of wine.

"No other Mission had so fine a church. It was one hundred and sixty feet long, fifty wide, and sixty high, with walls four feet thick. A tower at one side

San Luis Rey, seen through one of the Arches

held a belfry for eight bells. The corridor on the opposite side had two hundred and fifty six arches. Its gold and silver ornaments are said to have been superb.''

Even in its semi-ruined condition it is majestic and imposing. Over the chancel is a perfectly-proportioned dome, and on each side, and over the altar, are beautiful groined arches. Hanging high on the wall, on the right side facing the auditors, instead of on the left, is

a Byzantine wooden pulpit, which is reached by a quaint, narrow stairway from the chancel.

After the order of secularization reached San Luis Rey, Father Peyri decided that he must leave the scene, where, for thirty years, he had earnestly labored for the good of his loved Indians. Knowing how difficult it would be for him to get away from his "Indian children," "he slipped off by night to San Diego, hoping to escape without the Indians' knowledge. But, missing him in the morning, and knowing only too well what it meant, five hundred of them mounted their ponies in hot haste, and galloped all the way to San Diego, forty-five miles, to bring him back by force. They arrived just as the ship, with Father Peyri on board, was weighing anchor. Standing on the deck, with outstretched arms, he blessed them amid their tears and loud cries. Some flung themselves into the water and swam after the ship. Four reached it, and, clinging to its sides, so implored to be taken that the father consented, and carried them with him to Rome, where one of them became a priest."

Could a more affecting proof of the Indians' love for him have been given, or a higher tribute to the superlative worth of his spiritual work amongst them? Rest in peace! dear soul! in thy grave in far-away sunny Spain. Surely thy good deeds follow thee, and the memory of thy boundless love shall ever be a blessing to those who hear of thee in thy California field of labor, from which thou wast so rudely thrust!

The memory of Padre Zalvidea is also connected with San Luis Rey Mission. William Heath Davis relates that when he and James McKinlay were passing north once, they stopped at San Luis, and there found Zalvidea, "strong and healthy, although about eighty years of age. He spent most of his time in walking back and forth in the spacious piazza of the Mission, with his prayer-book open in his hand, saying his prayers, hour after hour. I stood, therefore, some time observing him, and every time he reached the end of the piazza he would give me a little side glance and nod of recognition, ar d say ' *Vamos si, senor*' a number of times in succession. Whenever he met me or anyone else through the day or evening he would make the same greeting, and never anything else. If anyone spoke to him he would listen attentively until the speaker had finished, apparently hearing and understanding everything that was said, but he made no reply other than the words I have quoted. During such interviews he would never look a person square in the face, but always gazed a little one side, round a corner as it were. One might have supposed he was demented from this singular conduct. I inquired if this was so of Mr. McKinlay, who had known him for ten years or more, and he replied that he was always the same; that he was so absorbed in his devotions that he did not care to hold any intercourse with the world or converse on worldly topics, but gave his whole life and attention to religion.

Father Zalvidea was much beloved by the people, who looked upon him as a saint on earth, on account of the purity and excellence of his character. Among his eccentricities was his custom, at meals, of mixing different kinds of food thoroughly together on one plate—meat, fish, vegetables, pie, pudding, sweet and sour—a little of everything. After they were thoroughly mingled, he would eat the preparation, instead of taking the different dishes separately, or in such combinations as were usual. This was accounted for as a continual act of penance on his part. In other words he did not care to enjoy his meals, and so made them distasteful; partaking of food merely to maintain existence. Whenever any ladies called on him, as they frequently did, to make some little present as a mark of their esteem, he never looked at them, but turned his face away, and extending his hand to one

SAN LUIS REY MISSION
DRAWN BY T. D. BEASLEY, AND PUBLISHED BY HIS PERMISSION.

side received the gift, saying, "*Vamos, si senora; muchas gracias.*" He never offered his hand in salutation to a lady. At times, in taking his walks for exercise in the vicinity of the mission, the priest was seen to touch his head lightly on either side with a finger, throw his hands out with a quick, spasmodic motion, and snap his fingers; as if casting out devils. On such occasions he was heard to exclaim "*Vete, satanas!*"—some improper thought, as he conceived, probably having entered his mind."

Whatever one may think of the action of the devout and venerable padre, his intense earnestness to lead the best life manifested to him is an example for the world to honor and emulate. Would there were more men filled with his earnest endeavor.

In 1892, it was determined to repair the Mission and have it occupied by the Franciscan order, and for this purpose Father O'Keefe of the Santa Barbara Mission, was sent to San Luis Rey to superintend its restoration. For months the work had been going forward, and on May 12, 1893, the formal dedication of the re-established Mission occurred with all due ceremony. The bishop of the diocese was present, together with the Vicar-General of the Franciscan order from Mexico, and other dignitaries. The ceremonies were as near as could be made like those of over a century ago, and, in the church, were three old Indian women, who had heard the original dedication services, where Padres Santiago and Peyri were the officiating clergymen.

Much has been done, under Father O'Keefe's intelligent supervision, towards arresting the decay of the old buildings, and so completely restoring them, that they will again be suited for Divine worship. A brick kiln occupies a portion of the interior quadrangle, and close by is a modern windmill, pump and water tank—rather incongruous they seem, in such a place, and yet useful and necessary. The dome over

Through the Old Garden Arch at San Luis Rey

the chancel has been effectively restored, in accordance with the original designs, and several of the walls repaired with imported brick. But the freight on them was so high that Father O'Keefe began the burning of his own brick, and he is now quite successful. The church has been re-roofed, and excavation of the corridors is now taking place.

Opposite the church several wooden buildings have been erected for the temporary, and, possibly, permanent occupation of those who come to be trained in the work of the Franciscans, and San Luis Rey, like Santa Barbara, is now educating priests instead of Indian savages.

With the delightful courtesy, so well known to visitors at Santa Barbara, Father O'Keefe left his other, and doubtless onerous, duties, to show myself and friend around, on a visit paid in October, 1894. We drove from Oceanside on a beautiful afternoon. After gradually rising from the ocean level, we came to a ridge from which a lovely view of a valley with mountains beyond, spread out before us. Yonder in the distance, in the valley, we could clearly see the mission, on a slight elevation, the river to the right, the valley and mountains to the left, the brown and white of the buildings, the exquisite green of the valley, the reddish gray and brown of the mountains combining to make a picture as full of harmony in color as Chopin's Nocturnes are full of harmony in sound. As we approached nearer we talked of the "gone by days" of Peyri, and Zalvidea, and Serra, of the sad demoralization of the Indians after the decree of secularization, and then, reverently and gladly we entered the sacred precincts. The signs of vigorous, though careful, restoration were most pleasing, and it is to be hoped that nothing will be allowed to stand in the way of a thorough completion of the work, under such careful and competent guidance as that of the Rev. Father O'Keefe.

While its history in the past is sad, there is comfort in the outlook for its future.

To reach San Luis Rey the visitor goes by rail on the Surf Line of the Santa Fe System, to the town of Oceanside, eighty-five miles from Los Angeles. Single fare, $3.15 ; round trip, $5.65. On Sundays, returning the same day, a special round trip rate of $3.00, from Los Angeles and return, is given. Going Saturday and returning Monday, a round trip ticket may be obtained for $4.00.

From here it is four miles drive to the Mission, and all information regarding conveyances will cheerfully be furnished by Mr. Peiper, mine host of the Oceanside Hotel.

CHAPTER XXI.

SAN ANTONIO DE PALA.

When at San Luis Rey, the interested visitor should endeavor to drive the eighteen or twenty miles further, necessary to bring him to the picturesque structure of San Antonio de Pala. It is not properly a mission, but merely a chapel, or branch of San Luis Rey, founded by Padre Peyri for the greater convenience of his beloved Indians, especially those who lived in the mountains. There were no buildings for neophytes as at the other Missions; nothing but a chapel and and a few scattered corrals. All readers of Mission literature are familiar with the picturesque belfry of Pala, crowned with a huge cactus, grown from a seed some passing breeze doubtless lodged in the adobe tower, where nourishing moisture fed it into active life.

The two bells, suspended in the little tower, still call the Indians from the surrounding hills to worship, and most fortunate is that visitor who can be present on one of these solemn occasions.

The building is long, narrow, low and dark, with adobe walls and rough beams set in them to support the roof, under which are layers of canes and tubes. Rude paintings cover the walls and other ornaments are a life-sized image of Antonio Palo, the warrior and priest from whom the mission takes its name, and a wooden statue of "St. Louis, King of France," which is held in profound reverence by the Indians, and on feast days is adorned with trappings and borne at the head of the procession of believers in the true faith. The floor is of brick, cracked and worn in recesses, copper and brass utensils evidently very old and dented from use, excite the curiosity of the visitor. They play a part still on days of ceremonial observance. The oaken door is plated with iron and stoutly riveted. While the walls are yet secure, the storms of winter are playing havoc with them, and, unless properly preserved, these picturesque ruins will soon be beyond all further help.

There is still an Indian settlement near Pala. Once or twice a month a priest from San Diego comes there and holds services for the Indians in this building, and they occasionally have a big celebration.

There are two old Indians, a man and a woman, who guard it quite zealously. A friend writes to me: "When I was there the figure of the patron saint, Pala, (which, by the way, was made by the Indians themselves out of the native clay) had a drawn thread handkerchief tied around his neck. Upon speaking of it I was told it had been placed there by an Indian woman who was suffering with a very bad cold, and she had thus protected the neck of the Saint with this handkerchief of her own make, hoping thereby to secure relief from her ailment. Pala also had several suits of clothing on, one over the other. The Indians dress him in one set of garments, and when a change is desired, instead of removing the suit he is then wearing they simply place the next one on.

There are two other statues here, one of San Luis, the patron of the San Luis Mission. The story goes that after the decree of secularization, when the soldiers came to take possession of, and incidentally to loot, the San Luis Rey Mission, a lot of Indians came down one night from their mountain retreat at Pala, stole these two statues from the sleeping soldiers, and with a few other articles held sacred, brought them to Pala and safety, where they ever since have been. They are nearly life size and are made of olive wood, said to have been carved in, and brought from, Spain.''

Tourists desiring to visit Pala can obtain accommodation at the house of Mr. Beale, who lives near the historic buildings, and who is the storekeeker for all the surrounding mountain region. This would be an interesting side trip for the tourist, as, in addition to the mission, the neighboring Indian villages would permit of a study of their home life and surroundings. The country is also quite picturesque, and the drive from Oceanside a pleasant one, easily made in a day.

CHAPTER XXII.

SANTA YNEZ.

In order to have a Mission nearer to the rancheros of twenty-seven baptized families, than Santa Barbara, the priests of that Mission made the request that a new establishment be made in a suitable location.

Accordingly on September 17, 1804, Comandante Carrillo, with nine soldiers from the Santa Barbara presidio, a large number of neophytes from that Mission and Purisima, under the guidance of Padres Jose Calzada and Jose Gutierrez, reached the appointed spot, and with the regulation ceremonies, solemnly dedicated a new Mission to St. Agnes, the beautiful virgin and martyr. One hundred and twelve persons were immediately enrolled on the books,—the members of the twenty-seven families before referred to.

The first church was so shattered by the earthquake of 1812, that a new edifice had to be constructed. On Independence Day, July 4, 1817, it was dedicated, and from that day fortune seemed to smile more frequently upon her affairs. Although the Indian population began to decline, her flocks and herds multiplied rapidly, and in 1831, or thereabouts, according to Davis, Santa Ynez Mission owned 20,000 cattle, 1,500 horses and mares, and 10,000 sheep.

In 1824, many of the Indians, both of this and other missions, became discontented, insubordinate and finally rebellious. More than a thousand Indians attacked the missionaries and killed and wounded several of their defenders. It is said "they could easily have captured the place if it had not been for the contagious fears of many escaped converts, who were overwhelmed with dread at the sound of chanting, the solemn ringing of the bells, and the sight of the priests armed with carnal weapons."

During this struggle many of the buildings were partially destroyed, and they have never been rebuilt. Santa Ynez is reached by stage or private conveyance from Santa Barbara.

CHAPTER XXIII.

SAN RAFAEL.

In 1817, owing to a frightful mortality in San Francisco, Lieutenant Sola suggested that, possibly, a move across the bay, where inland breezes would take the place of the ocean winds, might be beneficial to those who were still sick. The suggestion was adopted, and on December 14, 1817, a Mission was founded by Padre Luis Taboada at San Rafael.

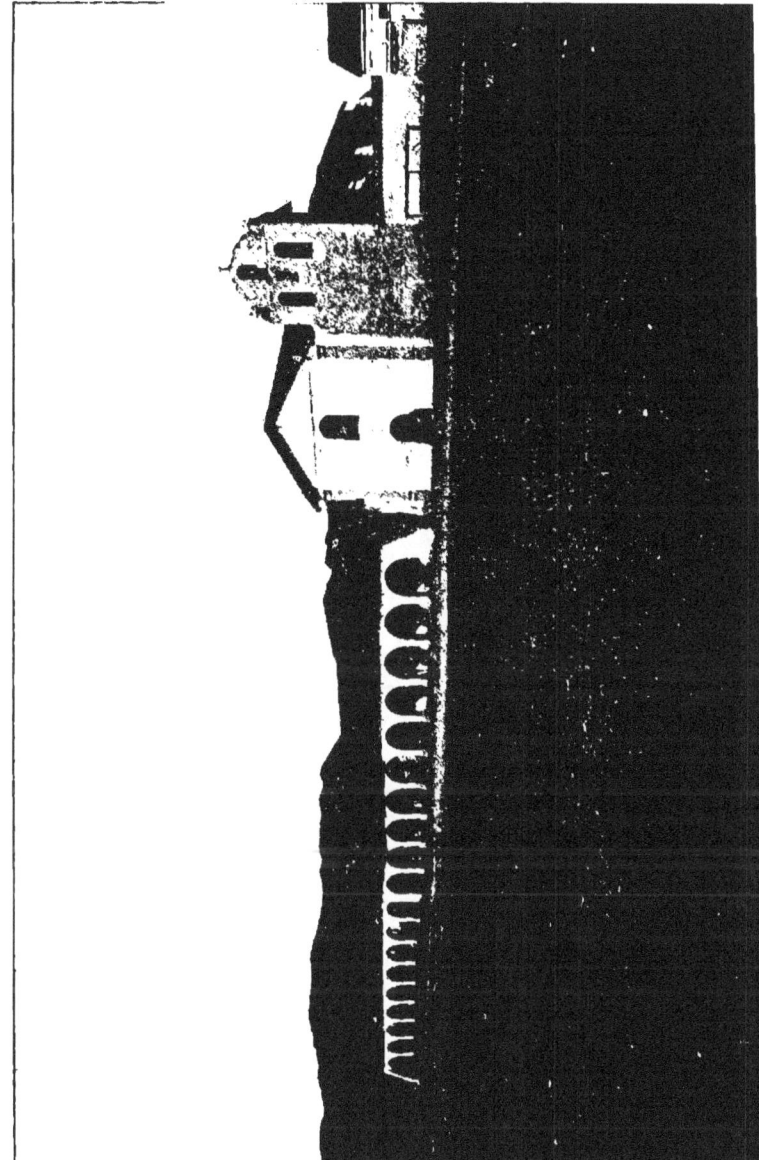

But little more than a memory remains today of San Rafael Mission. It is reached by the North Coast R. R. from San Francisco.

CHAPTER XXIV.

SAN FRANCISCO SOLANO.

This, the last of the Missions, was founded on Passion Sunday, April 4, 1824. and formally dedicated to the patron Saint of the Indies—San Francisco Solano.

It was but short-lived owing to having its inception when the true missionary spirit was on the wane. The building was only a temporary one, and it has long crumbled away, until now, nothing but its memory remains.

CHAPTER XXV.

LOS ANGELES CHAPEL.

Though not properly a Mission, the old church of Los Angeles has long been a source of great interest to the tourist, hence a brief account of its foundation will not be out of place.

In 1811 authority was gained for the erection of a chapel in Los Angeles for the benefit of the old soldiers who had long and faithfully served the King of Spain, and in August, 1814, Padre Gil, of San Gabriel, laid and blessed the corner stone. Nothing further, except the laying of the foundation, was accomplished until 1818, when the site was changed to its present location. In 1819 seven barrels of brandy and five hundred cattle were contributed towards the building fund, and by the end of 1820 the walls were raised to the window arches. Los Angeles, at this time, had a population of about 650, and an appeal was made to the governor in 1818, and through him to the viceroy, that the veterans who had spent their manhood's years in fighting for the king, and were now living in Los Angeles, ought not to be deprived of spiritual consolation and instruction any longer. But no priest or chaplain was sent to them. In 1822 or 1823 the chapel was finally completed, and formally dedicated on the 8th of December, 1822.

CHAPTER XXVI.

SANTA MARGARITA CHAPEL.

Another of these chapels was built at Santa Margarita, in San Luis Obispo county. It was undoubtedly built for the accommodation of those Indians who dwelt on the rancheria too far away to receive instruction regularly. It was built of stone but only dilapidated ruins now remain. The beauty of the region, possibly, was one of the sources of attraction to the traveler, for in 1862, J. Ross Browne wrote in Harper's Monthly:

"Next day I struck into the valley of Santa Margarita. I shall never forget my first impression of this valley; encircled by ranges of blue mountains were broad, rich pastures, covered with innumerable herds of cattle; beautifully diversified with groves, streams, and shrubbery, castellated cliffs in the foreground as the trail wound downward; a group of cattle grazing by the margin of a little lake, their forms mirrored in the water; a mirage in the distance; mountain upon mountain beyond, as far as the eye

could reach, till their dim outlines were lost in the golden glow of the atmosphere. Surely a more lovely spot never existed upon earth."

CHAPTER XXVII.

"CUI BONO?"

One thought necessarily comes to all minds as the work of the Mission Fathers is contemplated in the present condition of the Indians. *Cui Bono?*—What is the good of it all?

Who can tell? Except that no good work can fail!

There is one thing certain, and that is, that comparison between even the wretched treatment the missions received at the hands of the Mexican Government, and that which they have received at the hands of this intelligent, Christian government, is all in favor of Mexico. To our shame be is said!

Whatever our opinion may be of the padres, we are all compelled to share in the eloquent words of John W. Dwinelle: "They,"—the padres—"at least would have preserved these Indian races, if they had been left to pursue unmolested their work of pious beneficence."

For the preservation of the Mission buildings, I am happy to state that a society has been organized, with a number of earnest, active spirits at its head. The object of the Association is "to create a fund to be used for the preservation of the Mission buildings of California." The fee of membership is one dollar per year, and I trust that all those of my readers who are interested in these marvelous memorials of heroic and earnest Christian endeavor, will put themselves in communication with Miss Kelso, Librarian of the City of Los Angeles, who is chairman of the executive committee of the association.

www.ingramcontent.com/pod-product-compliance
Lightning Source LLC
Chambersburg PA
CBHW031324160426
43196CB00007B/659